and reach valid conclus‍
the evidence.

The l‍

RADIO LISTENING IN AMERICA

RADIO LISTENING IN AMERICA

The People Look at Radio—Again

Report on a survey conducted by
THE NATIONAL OPINION RESEARCH CENTER
of the University of Chicago; Clyde Hart, director

Analyzed and interpreted by
PAUL F. LAZARSFELD *and* **PATRICIA L. KENDALL**
of the Bureau of Applied Social Research
Columbia University

NEW YORK
PRENTICE-HALL, INC.
1948

Bluem, 1980

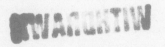

INTRODUCTION

During the last war, Frank Stanton conceived the idea of a periodic survey of the public's attitudes toward radio. Although much was known about specific listening habits, he felt that an important industry like radio should keep itself informed of what people know and feel about its general policies, the way it is organized and operated. Immediately after the armistice in the fall of 1945, a committee, headed by Dr. Stanton, developed a questionnaire and sent it into the field. The study was sponsored by the National Association of Broadcasters and conducted by the National Opinion Research Center, then at the University of Denver. By the end of 1946 the final report appeared under the title, *The People Look At Radio.** The co-author of that text, Harry Field, contributed greatly to the first study. His death in an airplane accident in Europe was a great shock and loss to all of his associates.

A year later, in the fall of 1947, a second survey went into the field, again sponsored by the NAB and again conducted by NORC, now at the University of Chicago. This time the questionnaire was worked out by a committee under the chairmanship of Hugh Beville. The senior author of the present report sat with this committee in all of its deliberations. The numerous questions suggested in these meetings were thoroughly tested; many of them were included in the final questionnaire; but, for reasons which are discussed in a special appendix to this volume, some had to be rejected. After the final questionnaire had been developed, it was sub-

* Published by the University of North Carolina Press, Chapel Hill, North Carolina.

iii

mitted to a group of social scientists who had previously criticized the first report. They made a number of improvements which were incorporated into the questionnaire on which the present report is based.

Special thanks are due Paul Sheatsley of the National Opinion Research Center who worked closely with the research committee, and whose research experience and ingenuity were indispensable throughout the study. Mr. Dick Baxter, research assistant at Columbia University's Bureau of Applied Social Research, was most helpful in many phases of the analysis. Miss Patricia Kendall took a larger and larger part in each subsequent revision of the present text until it was only fair to acknowledge her as co-author.

Paul F. Lazarsfeld

CONTENTS

RADIO LISTENING IN AMERICA

CHAPTER I

THE COMMUNICATIONS BEHAVIOR
OF THE AVERAGE AMERICAN

The mass media are a characteristic feature of present-day American life. From a few central agencies come the materials—the radio programs, the magazine stories, the films —which reach throughout the country. And for several hours of each day the average American finds himself a part of the audience for one or another of these mass media.

The present survey is essentially a study of the radio audience. However, it does provide an over-all picture of the general "communications behavior" of the American population. The nation-wide sample, reported on in these pages,[1] was not asked only about radio listening: There were questions on book-reading, movie attendance, the regularity of newspaper and magazine readership. These latter questions were not intended to yield detailed information. They do enable us, however, to distinguish between the "fans," "average consumers," and "abstainers" for any of the mass media, and they do make it possible for us to characterize these different groups. As a result we can relate radio listening to other types of communications behavior. We can determine whether there is any pattern of exposure, whether a "fan" of one medium is more or less likely to be a fan of other media as well. We can also study the relative importance of the various media for different subgroups in the population.

The classification of respondents into fans, average consumers, and abstainers is, of course somewhat arbitrary. This

[1] The characteristics of the sample and the reliability of results reported in this text are discussed in Appendix B.

I

can best be seen by comparing the information on movie-going and radio-listening given in Table 1. When we consider that a quarter of our sample saw four or more movies in one month, it does not seem unreasonable to consider a person who saw none as an abstainer, even though he may visit the movies six or seven times a year.

TABLE I

MOVIE-GOING AND RADIO-LISTENING BEHAVIOR

Number of Movies
Seen in Previous Month:

No movies	39%
1–3 movies	37
4 or more movies	24
Total	100%

Amount of Radio Listening
on Average Weekday Evening:

Less than 1 hour	26%
1–3 hours	49
3 or more hours	25
Total	100%

The classification of our respondents according to their amount of radio listening is more arbitrary.[2] Actually, only 5 per cent say that they never listen to the radio in the evening. An additional 21 per cent indicate that their evening listening is confined to less than an hour. Strictly speaking, then, this 21 per cent cannot be called abstainers, for they are reached by the radio. But, again, when we consider the more

---

[2] In this as well as in following discussions, our analysis of radio-listening behavior is based on the 91% of our total sample who reported that they owned radios in working order.

avid radio listeners, the persons who spend several hours an evening beside their radios, those who listen an hour or less can hardly be placed in the same category. They are light listeners, at least so far as evening listening is concerned. (Daytime radio listening will be discussed in a later section of this chapter.)

In both of these cases it is the extremes of behavior in our sample which enable us to distinguish between the fans and the abstainers. In neither case should the proportions within each category be taken too literally. Another classification scheme would yield a different distribution of "fans" and "abstainers."

There were no such problems of classification with regard to book and magazine readership. The respondents were asked only whether they read "any magazines regularly" and whether they happened to have read "any books during the last month." The information yielded by these questions is presented in Table 2. Incidentally, the figures reported here correspond fairly closely to those obtained in other surveys.[3]

TABLE 2

BOOK AND MAGAZINE READERSHIP

Book reading:
Read no books during past month.............	74%
Read at least one book during month..........	26
Total..................................	100%

Magazine reading:
Read no magazine regularly..................	39%
Read at least one magazine regularly..........	61
Total..................................	100%

[3] A review of other studies is currently being carried out for the Public Library Inquiry by Bernard Berelson, dean of the Graduate Library School at the University of Chicago.

Newspapers will not be included among the mass media to be discussed, for fully 90 per cent of the respondents in our sample say that they usually read a daily newspaper. It is true, of course, that newspaper reading may mean very different things for different people: Some readers just glance at the headlines; others carefully study the editorials, the feature articles, and so on. But a minimum reading of daily newspapers is so general a habit that no further analysis is possible here.

Overlapping Audiences

The four media with which we shall be concerned fall into two distinct groups. On the one hand there are those that require definite skills: One must be able to read before he can join the audience for books or magazines. But the readers of the two printed media are not always the same people. Books are more difficult to read than magazines, and, since they are more expensive, they are less easily accessible. It is not surprising, then, that almost every book reader is also a magazine reader, whereas the reverse is by no means true. These facts are shown in Table 3. The total number of magazine readers are found in the first two rows of this table; these figures indicate that only about one-third of the total read books as well as magazines. The total number of book readers, on the other hand, is listed in the first and third rows of Table 3, and here we find that the great majority of book readers, 80 per cent, read magazines in addition to books.

The few respondents (5 per cent of the total) who say that they read books but no magazines pose an interesting problem, for their behavior runs contrary to all expectations. And yet there was nothing in our survey to distinguish them from other readers. There are a few of them in all occupational groups, a few of them on all educational levels, a few of them in all geographical areas. Perhaps they have unusual tastes in reading matter, or perhaps they interpreted our questions in some special manner.

The second group of media, the movies and radio, re-

TABLE 3

RELATIONSHIP BETWEEN BOOK AND MAGAZINE READING

Combinations of book and
magazine reading:

Read both books and magazines..............	20%
Read magazines but do not read books.........	41
Read books but do not read magazines.........	5
Read neither books nor magazines.............	34
Total.................................	100%

quire no such skills as do books or magazines. They are more properly "spectator" media, in which the audience need do little more than watch or listen. Although there is a considerable number of people who prefer one of these forms of entertainment to the other, the audiences for movies and radio overlap to a large degree, much more than is the case with the printed media. From time to time there have been suggestions that the mass media might compete with each other for their audiences;[4] but when actual data have been available, they have indicated that the media tend to complement, rather than compete with, each other. It is true, of course, that television may change this situation in years to come.[5] But our survey contains no information on this point.

In the present study we found once again that the audiences for the different mass media are overlapping: A radio fan is likely to be a movie fan also, while, conversely, those

---

[4] Hugh M. Beville, Jr. "The Challenge of the New Media: Television, FM, and Facsimile," *Journalism Quarterly,* Vol. 25, pp. 3-11, 1948.

[5] For some speculations about the possible effects of television, see "Facts for the Future—The Broadcaster's Stake," a talk presented by Kenneth H. Baker at the Annual Convention of the National Association of Broadcasters, Los Aigeles, May, 1948.

persons who rarely go to the movies are likely at the same time to be light listeners. This is indicated in Table 4.

TABLE 4

PROPORTION OF LIGHT RADIO LISTENERS ACCORDING TO MOVIE ATTENDANCE

	NUMBER OF MOVIES SEEN IN PREVIOUS MONTH		
	No Movies	*1–3 Movies*	*4 or More Movies*
Proportion who listen to the radio less than one hour in the evening...............	31%	24%	18%

There is a similar relationship even between the printed and the spectator media. Table 5 shows that individuals who read no magazines regularly are likely to be light listeners and rare moviegoers.

TABLE 5

PROPORTION OF LIGHT RADIO LISTENERS AND RARE MOVIEGOERS ACCORDING TO MAGAZINE READERSHIP

	Do Not Read Magazines	*Read Magazines*
Proportion who listen to the radio less than one hour in the evening.	30%	22%
Proportion who saw no movies in the previous month...........	49	34

We may speculate for a moment as to the meaning of this general finding regarding communications behavior. What might account for the fact that a radio fan tends also to be a frequent moviegoer and a regular magazine reader? Two possibilities come to mind: Interest and opportunity. The man who is interested in world affairs finds that the radio will keep him abreast of the most recent events, that the newsreels will give him a pictorial summary of occurrences, and that the magazines will provide him with editorial comment and feature articles. Similarly, a woman interested in romantic fiction will find stories to suit her liking on the air, in movies, and in magazines. Or, to put it another way, the individual who is interested in a particular content will find that he can satisfy his interests better by exposing himself to all media than he can by confining his attention to one or two of them. Thus, if he has the time, he will divide it among the various media.

This raises the problem of opportunity. People who are absorbed in a specific activity, whether it is homemaking, a demanding job, or a time-consuming hobby, will have little time to expose themselves to any type of mass medium. Accordingly, they will be the abstainers, not only with regard to one or two, but all media. There may be factors other than interest and opportunity which bring about this pattern of high exposure to all media or no exposure (relatively speaking) to any. But whatever these influences may be and whatever their relative weight in producing the pattern, the fact itself is of obvious general interest and practical importance.

When we consider the relation of book reading and exposure to the spectator media, however, the results are no longer so clear-cut. As we see from Table 6, book readers are more likely to be movie fans, but there is no relation between book reading and radio listening: There are exactly as many radio fans, average consumers, and abstainers among the book readers as there are among the nonreaders. With

only the material that we have at hand, it is impossible to interpret this result.

The relationship between book reading and movie attendance deserves further comment, however. Table 6 shows that the audiences for these two media are characterized by the familiar overlapping: Book readers are more often frequent moviegoers, and, conversely, nonreaders are more often non-moviegoers. Although this may seem difficult to understand at first glance, developments in the communications industry suggest an explanation. In recent years the film industry has tended more and more to produce movies based on best-selling works of fiction and nonfiction. This apparently results in a kind of "double exposure": If people read a book which is later filmed, they go to see that movie and, con-

---

TABLE 6

RELATIONSHIP BETWEEN BOOK READING AND EXPOSURE TO SPECTATOR MEDIA

Amount of Evening Listening	Do Not Read Books	Read Books
None to 60 minutes	25%	25%
1–3 hours	50	48
Over 3 hours	25	27
Total	100%	100%

Movies Seen During Previous Month	Do Not Read Books	Read Books
No movies	44%	26%
1–3 movies	35	43
4 or more movies	21	31
Total	100%	100%

versely, they want to read the book on which a movie they have seen was based.[6] This mutual stimulation of book-reading and movie-going behavior deserves more detailed study than is possible in the present survey.

The Structure of the Mass Audience

There is a tendency, then, toward "all or none" behavior in the mass media field, but as is so frequently the case with such tendencies, there are a large number of exceptions. These exceptions, to which we now turn, are due largely to the fact that preferences for one or another of the media vary according to certain personal characteristics. Except for radio, each medium draws its most devoted audience from a different sector of the total population.

We should expect formal education to be one of the characteristics distinguishing "fans" and "abstainers." It is unlikely that persons whose schooling does not enable them to read with ease will be part of the audience for the printed media. These expectations are borne out by the data in Table 7: As level of formal education declines, so does readership of either books or magazines. Nearly all of the college-edu-

TABLE 7

PROPORTION OF MAGAZINE AND BOOK READERS
ACCORDING TO EDUCATION

	College	High School	Grade School
Proportion who read magazines regularly....................	86%	68%	41%
Proportion who read at least one book in previous month.......	50	27	11

[6] For some more concrete evidence of this "double exposure," see the section on *The Hucksters* in Chapter IV.

cated respondents report that they are regular readers of magazines; less than half of the respondents with grade-school education make that claim. The same educational differences characterize book-reading behavior. But Table 7 indicates also how few book readers are found in a cross section of the American population: Within each educational group there are fewer book readers than magazine readers.

For the two spectator media, movies and radio, education plays only a minor role. As we see in Table 8, there are only small and irregular differences between the various educational groups in amount of radio listening and movie attendance. It will be well to keep in mind, however, that so far as radio listening goes, the absence of educational differences refers only to the amount of time spent listening to the radio. We shall find in later chapters that there are marked differences in *what* is listened to and in attitudes toward radio.

TABLE 8

PROPORTION OF RADIO AND MOVIE FANS
ACCORDING TO EDUCATION

	College	High School	Grade School
Proportion who listen to the radio three hours or more in the evening	21%	29%	22%
Proportion who saw four or more movies in previous month	25	28	16

Although it is inherent in the nature of printed media that they will appeal primarily to highly educated people, it is not so immediately obvious what should characterize the audiences of the spectator media. Any observer of the American scene, however, who is asked to guess at the most distinguishing feature of the movie audience would at once think of age. And the materials in our survey would not disappoint him. Table 9 shows that the movie fans are found most generally among the young respondents, and that frequent movie going becomes less common as we proceed from one age class to the next. In fact, once the age of fifty is reached, it is non-movie going which is most characteristic.

TABLE 9

MOVIES SEEN DURING PREVIOUS MONTH
ACCORDING TO AGE

Movie Attendance	21–29	30–39	40–49	50–59	60+
No movies..........	19%	31%	36%	51%	73%
One movie..........	15	18	16	15	9
Two or three movies.	26	26	27	18	9
Four or five movies..	23	16	14	11	6
More than five movies	17	9	7	5	3
	100%	100%	100%	100%	100%

The relationship between age and movie attendance is probably one of the most spectacular findings in the whole field of communications behavior. Furthermore, it is a result which is confirmed in every study of movie going. For these reasons we have presented the data in considerable detail.[7]

It is not difficult to account for the fact that the movie fans are found among the young people. The teens and twenties are age periods of relatively few personal and social responsibilities, and therefore those people have more "free evenings." And since few young people have as yet developed definite intellectual goals, a free evening might just as well

[7] It might be relevant to point out here that none of our respondents was under 21 years of age. From other surveys of movie-going behavior, however, we know that the peak of movie attendance is at an even younger age—at about 19—so that, if anything, Table 9 underestimates the relationship between age and movie attendance.

be spent at the movies as in any other type of activity. Furthermore, movie going is a social activity (more than magazine reading, for example) through which the young people make social contacts which are important to them. Movie going is thus much more than mere entertainment. Whatever the content of the film, the experience of attending a movie probably plays an important role in the daily lives of young people.

As people grow older, however, they find their evenings filled with duties and plans, either imposed or self-assigned. In addition, movie going becomes more and more of an effort with increasing age: Having to travel to a theater, perhaps stand in line, and not return home until late are considerations which make movie going less enjoyable. Finally, older people, married and with a circle of friends of long standing, have less need for the kind of social activity represented by movie going.

There are additional data in our study to indicate the social context of movie attendance. We find, for example,[8] that single people, whatever their age, are more likely to be movie fans than married people. Furthermore, there is a marked sex difference in this respect. The single men in each age group, those who initiate social contacts, are more frequent moviegoers than are single women. Among the married people there is no such sex difference. Further evidence is contained in the radio program preferences expressed by different segments of the movie audience.[9] The fans, no matter what their age, choose popular and dance music, the kind of program suitable for social gatherings, much more frequently than do either the occasional or rare moviegoers.

The movies have an additional feature not characteristic of the other media. Magazines and radio programs come into

---

[8] See Appendix C, Table 3. These appendices have been prepared for readers interested in the more detailed findings of this survey. We shall have occasion to refer to them more frequently as the report proceeds.

[9] See Appendix C, Table 4.

the home; but we have to go to the movies. We should expect, therefore, that there will be fewer moviegoers where movies are less easily available. Table 10 shows that this is actually the case. We find less movie attendance in rural areas and in small towns than we do in the large cities where there is a movie theater around almost every corner.

TABLE 10

MOVIE ATTENDANCE ACCORDING TO SIZE OF COMMUNITY

Movies Seen During Previous Month	Metropolitan Districts Over One Million	Metropolitan Districts Under One Million	2,500 to 50,000	Rural Nonfarm (Under 2,500)	Farm
No movies......	32%	36%	36%	49%	52%
1-3 movies......	40	39	38	33	35
4 or more movies.	28	25	26	18	13
Total.......	100%	100%	100%	100%	100%

This table confirms what many students of communications behavior have emphasized before: The more easily available a medium is, the more people will expose themselves to it. We know, for example, that people are more likely to read the books within easy reach than they are to spend any time or effort searching for books in which they might be more interested.[10]

If education is such an important characteristic of the audience for the printed media, and age and residence for the movie audience, what characterizes the radio audience? Its most outstanding characteristic, it develops, is that it has no special features. During the evening, when most people are at home, there are no marked differences in listening among the

[10] D. Waples and R. W. Tyler, *What People Want to Read About: A Study of Group Interests and A Survey of Problems in Adult Reading.* Chicago: American Library Association and the University of Chicago Press, 1931.

major social groups. It is true that people with college training listen somewhat less, but the differences are small compared to those discussed so far. For the interested reader, others of these minor differences are summarized in the appendix.[11]

The term "mass," then, is truly applicable to the medium of radio, for it, more than the other media, reaches all groups of the population uniformly. As we have already indicated, this is true only in so far as *amount* of evening listening is concerned; we shall see presently that there are marked differences in what people listen to. Furthermore, we should remember that we have excluded newspapers from our discussion. Our data do not tell us how much time people spend reading the daily news, but if we take the mere fact of looking at a newspaper, of course, newspaper reading is as general as radio listening.

By confining our discussion to evening listening we have, so far, bypassed one very obvious fact. During the day most men are at work, and the large majority of married women are at home. Women, then, can more easily listen to the radio during the day, and they usually do. Because of this, one might modify the previous statements by saying that a sex difference is the outstanding characteristic of the radio audience. But this difference is due to the time schedules of men and women, rather than to any inherent appeals or characteristics of the medium.

We have data on the amount of time women spend listening to the radio in the morning and afternoon. This information permits us to return once more to the basic pattern of communications behavior. What should we expect from a comparison of women's listening during the three periods of the day? Is there a tendency to become satiated? If a woman listens a lot during one period of the day is she less likely to listen during another? Or does our law hold true here, too? Do women who listen a great deal during one part of the day also listen a lot at another?

[11] See Appendix C, Tables 5, 6, and 7.

The latter possibility is the correct one. Table 11, which actually contains three separate tables, shows the relationship between morning and afternoon listening, between morning

TABLE 11

THREE COMPARISONS OF LISTENING AT DIFFERENT PERIODS OF THE DAY
(Women Only)

a) Relation of Morning and Afternoon Listening

Morning Listening	AFTERNOON LISTENING		
	Less than One Hour	*1–3 Hours*	*3 Hours and Over*
Less than 1 hour.........	74%	35%	9%
1–3 hours..............	23	51	34
3 hours and over........	3	14	57
Total.............	100%	100%	100%

b) Relation of Morning and Evening Listening

Morning Listening	EVENING LISTENING		
	Less than One Hour	*1–3 Hours*	*3 Hours and Over*
Less than 1 hour.........	70%	51%	39%
1–3 hours..............	22	37	37
3 hours and over........	8	12	24
Total.............	100%	100%	100%

c) Relation of Afternoon and Evening Listening

Afternoon Listening	EVENING LISTENING		
	Less than One Hour	*1–3 Hours*	*3 Hours and Over*
Less than 1 hour.........	66%	53%	38%
1–3 hours..............	28	36	33
3 hours and over........	6	11	29
Total.............	100%	100%	100%

and evening listening, and between afternoon and evening listening. Examination of these figures shows again how strong the "all or none" tendency is in communications behavior. And, although the tendency exists in all three comparisons, it is particularly marked between morning and afternoon listening.

We can summarize our findings in this way: A radio fan in the morning is one in the afternoon and evening as well. Because of their psychological characteristics, their time schedules, and their lack of competing interests, women who are heavy listeners at one period of the day will tend to be radio fans throughout the day. Conversely, those women who cannot or do not want to listen much at one period will be light listeners consistently.

This ends our brief survey of general communications behavior. There are, of course, many further details, but these have all been relegated to an appendix so that the major trends would not become confused. However, the reader is invited to inspect the appendix with some care. It is interesting to observe what happens, for instance, when a variety of factors are combined and, thus, a variety of differences accumulated. We remember, for example, that three factors influenced movie attendance; ranked in the order of their importance these were age, residence, and sex. When we isolate the groups in which these three factors operate in combination, the differences in movie attendance become much greater. Among men between twenty-one and twenty-nine years of age living in large metropolitan areas, only 11 per cent fail to go to the movies; but among men fifty years or older living in rural areas, fully 75 per cent said that they had seen no movie during the previous month.[12] In the same way, the reader will find that age and education, when combined, make for interesting differences in exposure to the printed media.[13] It is only in regard to radio listening that these various combinations of

---

[12] See Appendix C, Table 8.
[13] See Appendix C, Tables 9 and 10.

characteristics fail to distinguish the fans from the abstainers.[14]

Because we have only these general indices of exposure for all media, our comparison cannot be carried any further. But this is a study of the radio audience primarily, and we therefore have detailed information on the radio-listening behavior of our sample of respondents. Continuing the discussion of communications habits, we turn to program preferences of the population. What are their favorite programs? What types of listening fare are particularly popular in different subgroups of our cross section? Have there been any changes in listening behavior over the last two years?

---

[14] See Appendix C, Tables 11 and 12.

CHAPTER II

PROGRAMS AND THEIR LISTENERS

Communications habits cannot be described solely in terms of quantity of exposure. It would be a mistake to assume that two individuals behave identically just because they see the same number of movies each month or listen to the same number of radio programs each evening. One of these individuals may see four western movies a month whereas the other sees four film biographies during the same period; one of them may spend an hour each evening listening to quiz and comedy programs, and the other spends the same amount of time listening to discussions of public issues and to news broadcasts. The *quality* of selections is a further dimension of movie or listening habits. What specific types of movies or radio programs are chosen? These two pieces of information, when considered together, provide a well-rounded picture of communications behavior. As we have already indicated, we were not able to ask about specific reading or movie selections, but we did ask a number of questions about preferences for different kinds of radio programs.

In this as well as in the earlier survey we asked each respondent the following question:

Here's a set of cards listing different kinds of radio programs. Would you mind looking through these cards, and telling me the types of programs you like to listen to in the daytime? Now which types of programs do you like to listen to in the evening?

The nature of the information which we obtained when we asked people what they like to listen to can best be brought out by a comparison with the well-known program ratings. A rating indicates, with more or less precision, how many people listen to a given program at a given time. But, for a number of reasons, such listening figures are only limited indices of radio preferences. If two equally fine programs are on the air at the same time, each may get only half as high a rating as it would if it had no competition. Secondly, a program broadcast at eight o'clock in the evening is likely to have an audience several times larger than that which it would get at three o'clock in the afternoon. Too, it is difficult to compare the audience ratings of two programs when one of them is a type frequently heard and the other is a type broadcast only rarely. And finally, no ratings are available for programs which are not commercially sponsored, although many of these are of special interest to the student of communications habits. Competition, time on the air, extent of supply, and sponsorship are at least four factors which limit the ability of audience ratings to provide information on attitudes toward radio programs. To this it must be added that ratings, usually obtained by telephone, ordinarily yield nothing beyond the total size of the audience and generally tell nothing about its composition—whether the bulk of listeners are young or old people, educated or uneducated.

The questions on general program preferences do much to cut through these difficulties. But as is so often the case in research, a method which avoids one type of limitation encounters others. Whether a person did or did not listen to a certain program can be established with a fair amount of accuracy. Whether he "likes to listen" to a specific program is a much looser question. On the one hand it can mean that he is enthusiastic about the program, or on the other hand it can mean that he listens to it only because nothing more desirable is available at that time.

Another problem is that some listeners experience difficulty in answering a question on program preferences. Table 12 shows that two factors are particularly important in this regard. People who spend a lot of time listening to the radio mention a larger number of favorite program types—this is as it should be. But ability to answer such a question is also dependent on level of formal schooling. Educated people can articulate their thoughts with greater ease, they are better able to discriminate between the different program types on the list shown them, and they have wider interests. As a result they mention more favorite programs than do the uneducated listeners. The differences are quite marked. Uneducated people who are light listeners mention only 3.6 favorite programs on an average; but educated people who are heavy listeners mention nearly twice as many, an average of 6.7.

TABLE 12

AVERAGE NUMBER OF FAVORITE PROGRAM TYPES ACCORDING TO EDUCATION AND AMOUNT OF EVENING LISTENING*

Amount of Evening Listening:	Grade School	High School	College
Less than 1 hour	3.6	4.1	4.8
1–3 hours	5.4	5.7	6.5
3 or more hours	6.3	6.5	6.7

* The figures in this table represent the average number of favorite programs mentioned by the designated groups of listeners.

There is a practical conclusion drawn from the information in this table which should be kept in mind. When we come to study the specific preferences of the educated and uneducated groups, we shall pay particular attention to those programs mentioned even slightly more frequently by the uneducated listeners. Because of their general inarticulateness, we should expect them to check all programs less frequently. Therefore, we shall consider even a small surplus statistically as well as psychologically significant. The reverse will hold true for a program checked more frequently by well educated listeners. There the differences will have to be large before we shall consider them worthy of special attention.

A final difficulty in asking about program preferences is the absence of a clearly established terminology for program types. Answers are somewhat dependent upon the wording of the question. If we ask about "radio plays," some listeners will think of daytime serials even if they are specifically mentioned in another part of the list. If the question is about

TABLE 13

THE CONSTANCY OF PROGRAM PREFERENCES*
(1947 compared with 1945)

	Daytime Preferences				Evening Preferences	
	MEN		WOMEN		TOTAL	
	1945	*1947*	*1945*	*1947*	*1945*	*1947*
News broadcasts.....	65%	61%	76%	71%	76%	74%
Comedy programs....	*	*	*	*	54	59
Popular and dance music............	15	23	35	39	42	49
Talks or discussions about public issues.	22	19	21	22	40	44
Classical music.......	12	11	23	20	32	30
Religious broadcasts..	19	22	35	41	20	21
Serial dramas........	7	6	37	33	*	*
Talks on farming.....	13	16	12	13	*	*
Homemaking programs	5	5	44	48	*	*
Livestock and grain reports............	14	17	6	10	*	*

* Figures do not add to 100% because more than one answer was permitted each respondent. The starred program types are not considered because of the infrequency with which they are heard at the designated times.

"radio plays completed in one program," the figures are somewhat different. Because of this fact, two studies can be compared only when they have used the same lists of program types.

The lists which we used in the earlier and present studies contained ten items which were identical. One outstanding fact emerges from a study of answers to these items. Where a comparison was possible, we find great constancy of listener preferences. Table 13 shows that with only minor exceptions, these program types are no more and no less popular today than they were two years ago.

General tastes apparently remain relatively unchanged over a two-year period. This fact is not surprising, but it is important to bear in mind. For we occasionally hear that a particular program type has gained in popularity, or that the ratings for a specific program have suddenly become higher. Such events are, of course, important for the broadcasters and sponsors involved, but they seem due largely to incidental

TABLE 14

ADDITIONAL PROGRAM PREFERENCES*

	DAYTIME PREFERENCES		EVENING PREFERENCES
	Men	Women	Total
Quiz and audience participation......................	15%	35%	56%
Complete dramas (other than mystery)................	*	*	46
Mystery programs.........	*	*	41
Semiclassical music........	13	28	33
Hillbilly and western music..	18	25	26
Sports programs...........	30	14	33

* Figures do not add to 100% because more than one answer was permitted each respondent. The starred items are not considered because of the infrequency with which they are heard at the designated times.

circumstances. The basic attitudes of listeners, uncovered in such a study of preferences, seem to change very slowly.

For the record we report answers to items which were either added in our present study or which were phrased differently as a result of our previous experiences.

Information on program preferences can be used to reveal not only the stability of radio tastes, but also differences between various sectors of the population. And the latter is perhaps the more interesting use. As we saw in the first chapter, all social groups spend approximately the same amount of time listening to the radio, but when we examine what it is they actually listen to, marked group differences appear. Now there are two ways in which we can approach these differences. On the one hand we can focus our attention on the social groups themselves. We can determine which program types are the particular favorites of men and which of women; we can find out what types have special appeal for educated listeners and which for uneducated; we can see whether city dwellers have different preferences from people living in rural areas; and so on. Or we can turn the question around and investigate the audiences for specific programs. Who listens to news broadcasts and who to quiz programs? Is the audience for classical music composed of different social groups than the audience for mystery shows? This latter approach was the one used in our earlier survey and, because the situation has changed so little, it would be pointless to repeat the analysis here. The reader who is interested in one or another program type can find the relevant information in our previous report.[1]

In this report we shall look at the listeners themselves, summarizing briefly the program preferences of different subgroups in the population. This leads us back to a more detailed consideration of the factors already discussed in Chapter I.

---

[1] See Paul Lazarsfeld and Harry Field, *The People Look at Radio*, Chapter III. Chapel Hill: The University of North Carolina Press, 1946.

Major Group Differences

The factor with most far-reaching implications is what is usually called socio-economic status. Everyone knows that some people have more power, more prestige, and more money than others. The difference between the underdog and the man in the social register is a well-known feature of daily life. But there is disagreement on the extent to which these social strata have become fixed in the American community. Some consider the classes of society fairly well established and rigid, whereas others think that many of the "little men" still have a chance to become "big shots." The corner grocer in a small community sometimes has more prestige with his fellow men than the town's richest citizen. But by and large it is recognized that society looks like a layer cake, and there is not much doubt as to who is on top and who is at the bottom.

The research student is also aware of social stratification. He expects to find more magazines, more refrigerators, and more Buicks in the upper strata; more children, more unemployment, and more Chevrolets in the lower strata.

It makes little difference which particular index is used to classify people into social layers. Any one of the four or five reasonably good measures yields about the same results in a survey on radio listening. For a number of reasons we shall use education as our index in the following discussion. On the lowest stratum we shall put those respondents who have not gone beyond grade school; those who have attended high school will form a middle group; and the third and top layer consists of people who have had at least some college education. For the country as a whole, about 55 per cent belong on the lowest level and about 12 per cent belong on the highest.[2]

---

[2] Table 13 in Appendix C has been prepared for statistically minded readers. This shows that a classification by education and a classification according to interviewers' ratings are really interchangeable. The well educated people are also the individuals with high

When we examine listening preferences, we find that there are a number of program types which are liked equally well by all strata. If the general inarticulateness of uneducated respondents is taken into account, we can say that comedy programs, news broadcasts, sports programs, and popular music cut across the socio-economic levels. The same is true for mystery stories, which were not specifically studied in the earlier survey, and to which we shall return presently. There is no doubt that a large proportion of the radio schedule is devoted to these five kinds of programs and that they are typical of American radio. Why should one stress the importance of social differences in taste, then?

Our answer is that social differences are significant because of the kinds of programs on which the various strata disagree. Programs of serious music and discussions of public issues are selected as favorites twice as frequently in the college group as in the grade school group.[3] In other words, the program types which reveal most marked differences in taste are those which have come to symbolize radio's cultural or educational mission. They are favorites of the highly educated listeners, but they hold relatively little appeal for listeners on the lower strata. This fact creates a dilemma for the broadcaster. In order to make his business a success, he needs large audiences, and, for obvious reasons, these are drawn mainly from less educated groups. He therefore feels that he cannot broadcast too many programs which have only limited appeal

---

ratings. This indicates that our findings would have been essentially the same had we used this other measure of socio-economic status for our classifications.

[3] See Table 14 in Appendix C. This table shows the program preferences of the radio audience divided into different educational and age groups. If we want to see whether there are any educational differences in listening tastes, we compare the college-educated respondents of one age group with the high school and grade school respondents of the same age. In other words, we compare the first, fourth, and seventh columns; the second, fifth, and eighth columns; or the third, sixth, and ninth columns. If, on the other hand, we want to study age differences, we examine the answers of the different age groups within any one educational class.

for uneducated listeners. But in satisfying one section of his audience, the broadcaster antagonizes another. The educated and articulate minority feel that they are neglected—they claim that they hear too few of the serious programs which are their favorites. In the course of our report we shall return repeatedly to this difficulty.

There are also a number of programs which are the particular favorites of the lower socio-economic strata. Conspicuous among these is hillbilly music, but the same pattern holds true for religious programs and for daytime serials as well.

Quiz programs, interestingly enough, are mentioned most frequently by respondents in the middle stratum, those who have attended high school but not college. This result is significant from a psychological point of view. We have found in previous studies that many listeners like quiz programs because they consider them informative. In our earlier survey a large number of listeners immediately mentioned quizzes when asked for examples of educational programs. It is easy to understand why this attitude is most prevalent among people with only a moderate amount of schooling. Individuals with college education have been trained to look for information in printed sources, whereas on the lowest educational level there are few people who have developed a desire to look for information. Quiz programs are therefore most valuable to the middle group: Occasionally they can learn something through a familiar medium.

Educational differences in program tastes are significant because they point to the broadcasters' dilemma. There is another factor—age—which produces equally marked differences even though these may be of less practical importance. Some of the age differences are easily understood: Young people like programs of dance music very much more than older people do; they like religious programs very much less. But there are other program types on which age differences cannot be anticipated so easily. What should we expect in connection with serious programs such as discussions of current events or concerts of classical music? Does it seem likely that young people, with high ambitions and their lives ahead of them, will take advantage of radio programs through which they might improve themselves? Or, does it seem more likely that their interest in social activities will be expressed in preferences for lighter radio fare. We know from other social researches that young people vote less frequently than their elders, and that they do not often read serious magazines or books. It turns out that the same general attitudes are revealed in their radio preferences. They mention classical music and forums as favorites considerably less frequently than do their parents. It is a matter of opinion whether the younger generation's lack of serious interests is "natural" or whether it should be viewed with regret. But the fact that serious interests develop only as we grow older is significant. Anyone anxious to understand the mood of our times must bear it in mind.

We also find different program preferences among men and women.[4] The average American woman, just like the average American youth, is not interested in current affairs. This fact has been discovered in so many areas of behavior that we are not surprised to find it reflected also in program preferences. And it is indeed reflected, for twice as many men like discussions of public issues and considerably more men are interested in evening news broadcasts. There is another sex difference which reveals equally clearly how some interests are defined by tradition as "male" and others as "female." Sports programs are chosen as a favorite by four times as many men as women; but it is more difficult to understand why men like comedy programs better than women do. There are other programs which have special appeal for women. In the daytime, of course, they have their serial dramas and their homemaking programs practically to themselves. But there are also evening programs which women are more inclined to include among their favorites—these are nonserial dramatic programs, quiz shows, and semiclassical music.

The recent war created a new social group—veterans. We might suppose that their experiences in the armed forces

---

[4] See Table 15, in Appendix C.

influenced their attitudes and interests; perhaps they became more serious-minded, more interested in current affairs. But when we study their program preferences, we find that they are very similar to nonveterans of comparable age.[5] Veterans are slightly more interested in forums on public issues, but the differences are small. The only program type which shows any substantial difference is sports programs. For reasons which are difficult to understand immediately, veterans like these programs very much more than do nonveterans.

Finally, we can note that there are some urban-rural differences in program preferences. Interestingly enough, farmers and city dwellers disagree most markedly in their musical tastes. Programs of classical and semiclassical music are much more popular in cities than on farms, and, conversely, hillbilly music is much better liked by people in rural areas.[6] Farmers and city dwellers do not differ in their attitudes toward popular dance music. But what about nonmusical programs? What about comedy programs, for example? Most of them originate in large cities and frequently deal with city dwellers. We may wonder, therefore, whether farmers appreciate this kind of humor. Apparently they do. In fact, there are only minor and irregular disagreements on nonmusical programs. Dramas, mystery programs, and sports programs are somewhat less popular in rural areas; religious programs are somewhat better liked on farms. For the most part, however, there are few and only minor differences in taste with regard to nonmusical programs.[7]

It is important to recognize that we have only been talking about broad *types* of programs—comedy as compared with forums on public issues, classical music as compared with

---

[5] See Table 16, in Appendix C.

[6] See Table 17, in Appendix C. These differences remain when education is held constant.

[7] This statement is not absolutely correct. There is one program type—reports on livestock and grain—which is much more popular among farmers. Since they are the only listeners who have any real interest in such programs, however, we cannot consider this a difference in taste.

religious programs. If we had further information on specific programs within each broad type, we would undoubtedly find additional social differences in taste. Farmers, for example, will prefer radio dramas when they take place in a rural setting; soldiers will like comedies about life in the armed services; parents will be particularly interested in serious programs about child psychology. These facts, established in many previous studies, can be explained in the following way: People like to read stories or see movies or hear radio programs which deal with familiar situations. They are particularly interested in content which in some way agrees with their own experiences. Thus, whatever their over-all attitudes toward serious programs, or comedies, or any other general program type, various social groups will like some specific comedies better than others, and some serious programs less well than others.

Further Observations on Radio Preferences

We could go on with this kind of investigation, studying the listening preferences of married and single people, of professionals as compared with white collar workers, and so on. But it is doubtful that this would advance us very far, because the kind of analyses which we have just reported always lead back to one basic problem. General characteristics such as age, sex, and education permit us to say what kinds of programs are popular in which groups. This is useful information, and we do not discount its importance in any way. It enables the broadcaster to schedule his programs so that they are on the air at times when people for whom they have special appeal are available. Such information also helps sponsors decide how to use their advertising funds most effectively. But knowing that men seem to like sports programs tells us nothing about the man who turns off his radio when he hears a sports announcer. Knowing that college-educated listeners like classical music reveals nothing about why some college professors detest such music. In other words, idiosyncrasies of taste cannot be investigated satisfactorily when all we know about the listeners is that they belong to a specified social group. We need more detailed information on their psychological make-up.

Some efforts to study psychological differences in taste have already been made, but none of these attempts has ended very successfully. We know, for example, that the daytime audience is sharply divided on the issue of daytime serials. About half of the women who are available listen to one serial after another; the other half avoid them assiduously. In order to determine whether these two groups of women differ in personality, in their modes of life, or in any other way, they have been subjected to batteries of psychological tests and they have been interviewed intensively. But so far the results of these studies have been negative, for no differences have been found.[8]

Yet people do not listen indiscriminately to every kind of radio program; they show consistent listening patterns. This, in turn, indicates that their radio tastes are determined by some more basic psychological factors. How can we go about isolating these different elements of taste? The present survey was not designed with this problem in mind, and we can therefore do little more than indicate the path that might be followed. In future investigations we should perhaps concentrate on the *interrelations* of program preferences. One simple example will help to clarify what we mean. Let us consider mystery programs and daytime serials. Do these two types of programs appeal to the same or to different elements of taste? It is hard to say. Both program types have one major feature in common—they both contain elements of suspense. We might suppose, therefore, that a listener who likes one will also like the other. But they also differ in one major respect—daytime serials are concerned with domestic problems and situations; mystery programs are not. We might just

---

[8] See Herta Herzog, "Psychological Gratifications in Daytime Radio Listening," in *Readings in Social Psychology* (edited by T. Newcomb and E. Hartley). New York: Henry Holt & Company, Inc., 1947.

as easily expect, therefore, that someone who likes one type will dislike the other.

By studying the actual relationship between the two programs, then, we can perhaps determine which of the appeals—domesticity or suspense—seems to be dominant in preferences for daytime serials. If serial listeners also like mystery programs, we can say that suspense seems to be the more important appeal. And, conversely, we can say that individuals who express a preference for either mystery or serial programs like suspense. If, on the other hand, it turns out that the two programs have a negative relationship, that is, if an individual who likes one type dislikes the other, we can say that the more important appeal of daytime serials is their concern with domestic problems. We can also say that someone who likes serials is apparently interested in domestic problems, whereas someone who likes mystery programs is interested in less familiar situations.

The actual data from the present survey are reported in Table 15. In order to make certain that all persons included in our analysis were available for listening throughout the day, we excluded any women who did not report both daytime and evening listening. The remaining 1,528 women were then

TABLE 15

RELATIONSHIP BETWEEN MYSTERY PROGRAMS AND DAYTIME SERIALS
(Women Only)

	Like Mysteries	Do Not Like Mysteries	Total
Like serials............	276	265	541
Do not like serials......	356	631	987
Total.............	632	896	1,528

classified in four ways, depending on whether or not they mentioned either mysteries or serials among their favorite programs.

It turns out that women who like serials also like mysteries. But in order to study how strong the relationship actually is, we need an "index of overlapping listening." The coefficient which we shall use has an upper limit of 1.0 when everyone who likes one program also likes the other type; it has a lower limit of 0, signifying complete absence of overlap, when there is no one who likes both types.[9] In the present example, we find a value of .472, indicating a moderately high relationship. We can conclude therefore that both serials and mysteries make some appeal to a taste for suspense, and that listeners who select these programs as their favorites have such tastes.

This index of overlapping listening permits us to carry our analysis one step further. With it we can study what might be called the "psychological propinquity" of different programs. In order to illustrate this let us consider the musical preferences of our respondents. Our program list contained four musical items: Classical music, semiclassical music, popular dance music, and hillbilly music. We can be certain that classical and semiclassical music will have a fairly high index of overlapping. But what about the other two types? Which is psychologically "nearer" to classical music—popular dance tunes, or hillbilly songs? We could hardly tell in advance, but Table 16 suggests an answer.

It turns out, then, that hillbilly music is psychologically most distant from classical music, for these two types show

---

[9] Our index can be described in the following way. 51% (or 276/541) of the serial listeners also like mystery programs. Similarly, 44% (or 276/632) of the people who like mystery programs say also that they like serials. The index value is found by taking the square root of the product of these two percentage figures (this is what statisticians call a "geometric mean"):

$$\sqrt{\frac{276 \times 276}{541 \times 632}} = \frac{276}{\sqrt{541 \times 632}} = .472$$

TABLE 16

OVERLAPPING OF MUSICAL TASTES

	Classical	Semi-classical	Popular	Hillbilly
Classical.........	x	.567	.410	.253
Semiclassical.....	.567	x	.469	.261
Popular..........	.410	.469	x	.409
Hillbilly.........	.253	.261	.409	x

the lowest amount of overlap. If the reader studies Table 16 carefully, he will see that the figures are quite consistent: They suggest that musical tastes vary along a kind of psychological continuum, with classical music at one extreme and hillbilly music at the other.

In addition to its general theoretical interests, such a result also has practical implications. Station managers are becoming increasingly interested in the idea of "mood"-programming. They try to have programs which give similar psychological gratifications adjacent to each other, so that there is not too much audience turnover at the end of each quarter- or half-hour. The kind of analysis which we have just suggested will help them schedule programs most effectively. Table 16, for example, indicates the best order in which to present different musical programs. Analyses of overlapping listening should be pursued further in future studies, but in order to proceed along these lines, it will be necessary to develop lists of program items designed to answer clear-cut problems. With the materials available at the present time we can do little more than outline and illustrate the procedure.

As more psychological approaches develop, it should not be forgotten that tastes and preferences are partly dependent on external circumstances. At the beginning of this chapter we emphasized the constancy of program tastes. Much of this is due to the fact that there were few changes in the general radio situation during the interval between the two surveys. It is true that quiz programs and particularly "give-away" shows have increased both in number and in popularity during the past year; but at the time when our second sample was interviewed, these developments were only getting under way. Our data were obtained before there had been any marked changes in the program types, the quantities of each type available, or the main formulae around which they were built.

When there is a marked change in the environment, however, people's reactions seem to vary. This is indicated by answers to a question which was included in both the earlier and the present surveys. At both times, all listeners were asked:

> Where do you get most of your daily news about what is going on—from the newspapers or the radio?

The conclusion of the war has changed the role of the two most important mass media. During the war everyone was eager to hear about new events as soon as they occurred. Speed and immediacy were what mattered most, and here radio had undisputed advantages. Now that the war is over, it is possible that news has become less vital to the average

TABLE 17

RELATIVE IMPORTANCE OF RADIO AND NEWS-
PAPERS AS SOURCE OF DAILY NEWS

Get most of news from:	1945	1947
Newspapers............................	35%	48%
Radio.................................	61	44
Don't know............................	4	8
	100%	100%

citizen or that he is likely to think so; therefore, we can expect the relative importance of radio to have declined somewhat. As Table 17 indicates, this is indeed the case.

We might mention in passing that the kinds of people preferring one or the other medium have not changed. It is still the women, the less educated people, the poorer people, and the heavy listeners who are most dependent on radio for their news.

But what is most important in the present context is that a constancy of taste reflects partly a constancy of supply and of other external conditions. Important changes in the environment are followed by noticeable changes in attitude. This finding sets the stage for a more detailed consideration of the use of radio for cultural purposes. When studying program preferences, we found little change in attitudes toward serious programs of classical music or forum discussions. Because the matter is so important, it seems desirable to pursue it further. We are particularly interested in finding out whether attitudes toward such serious programs could be modified by actions and policies of the broadcaster. What does the present study permit us to say on this subject?

Learning From Radio

It is well known that educational programs have low ratings. Even the most successful discussions of public affairs or the most effective dramatizations of historical events have only small audiences when they are compared with major entertainment programs. There are a number of possible explanations for this fact. It may be that the American public is just not interested in serious programs, and that the appropriate interests can never be developed. It is also possible that the relative unpopularity of serious radio fare indicates that there are too few of these programs at present, that they are scheduled at inconvenient times, or that their broadcast time is shifted so that it is difficult for them to build up their audiences.[10] In preceding paragraphs we found that radio tastes are somewhat dependent on external factors; supply is certainly one of these factors. For a variety of reasons, the American radio schedule is now devoted largely to entertainment programs, and these are actually the most popular listening fare. If there were a larger number of serious programs, and if these were carefully written and conveniently scheduled, they, too, might find a more receptive audience. Increased supply might be followed by increased interest.

It may be that current program ratings are misleading, for they may underestimate the number of people who would listen to serious programs if more of them were provided.

TABLE 18

"Of course, most people listen to news broadcasts on the radio. But which one of these statements best describes the way you yourself use the radio for other types of programs?"

A. I listen to the radio mostly for entertainment and very seldom listen to serious or educational programs.................................... 26%

B. I like to listen to both serious and entertainment programs, and I'm satisfied with what I get now.. 52

C. I like to listen to both serious and entertainment programs, but I wish there were more serious programs.................................... 20

Don't know.............................. 2

Total................................. 100%

---

[10] The timing of serious programs is obviously an important consideration in their popularity. Both the hours at which they are broadcast and the consistency with which they are scheduled at these times will have an effect on their ratings. Unfortunately, however, very little is known about the timing of serious programs at the present time. A comprehensive analysis of program schedules, studying both the timing and the permanence of broadcast schedules, remains to be carried out.

Any conclusive answer to these questions would require a program of coordinated research, including, perhaps, a number of experimental studies. We made an effort in the present survey to measure the single factor of interest, distinct from questions of supply, of scheduling, of actual behavior, and so on. These latter factors remain to be studied in future investigations. The question which we used was decided on after considerable experimentation; its wording and the distribution of answers which it received are presented in Table 18.

Twenty per cent of our cross section express a desire for more serious programs; 52 per cent say they listen to educational programs and are satisfied with the present supply. Our interest centers on the third group. If it is true that 20 per cent really want more serious programs, there is indeed a large potential audience. But two questions immediately arise. One is whether such statements can be taken at face value, or whether they are like avowals of "being against sin." The second question concerns the characteristics of people who request more serious programs.

Let us begin with the second point. One might suspect that these 20 per cent come mainly from highly educated groups. They would, as a matter of course, favor more serious programs, but it might be that they recommend such programs for "other people" rather than for their own benefit. They themselves have books and other sources of information, but they might very easily feel that it would do the other fellow a lot of good if more serious programs were available to him. If this turned out to be the case, we would attach little importance to our finding, for the broadcaster could not be sure that anyone would listen to his serious programs, even if he offered a larger number of them.

But the actual data show that the 20 per cent are very evenly distributed among all educational strata. Graph I classifies people according to their education and their purposes in listening. Taking our total sample as 100 per cent, we find that there are 6 per cent who have gone to college and want more serious programs. But we also find 6 per cent who have only gone to grade school and who express the same desire. In other words, the two extreme educational groups contribute equal numbers of people to the market for serious pro-

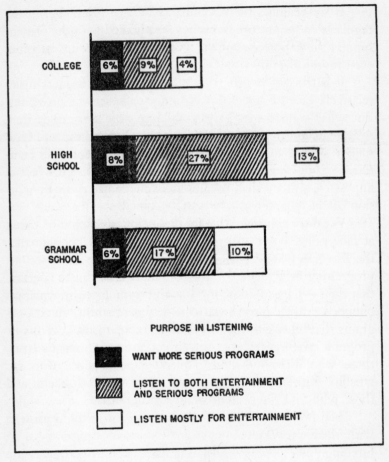

GRAPH I

Market for serious programs in different educational groups.

grams. On the high school level there is an even greater number of people. This indicates once more, incidentally, that it is respondents with moderate education who are especially interested in adult education. They have probably had enough schooling to know its value, but not enough to be completely satisfied. Radio is therefore particularly important for them; it is a medium for self-improvement as well as for entertainment.

If we examine the respondents who say that they listen regularly to serious programs but are satisfied with the present supply, the importance of the lower educated groups becomes even more obvious.

It is true, of course, that better educated listeners make relatively more requests for an increase in serious programs. But what concerns us here is absolute numbers rather than relative proportions. In this respect the grade school and high school people make a good showing—they represent two-thirds of the total market for serious programs. This fact is impressive and we shall review its implications at the conclusion of this chapter.

We must consider whether these requests should be taken at face value. If we are to do so, we must make certain that the listeners who say they would like to hear more serious programs give evidence of meaning it. We must make certain that their expressed desire is consistent with other information obtained in their interviews. One lead is to study which programs they check as their favorites. Table 19 lists the major program preferences for our three groups of respondents, those who listen mostly for entertainment, those who are satisfied with the present supply of serious programs, and those who find the present supply too limited.

The preferences of all groups are remarkably consistent with their answers to our general question on purposes in listening. The people who want more serious programs are actually more interested in the specific program types which symbolize serious radio—forums and classical music. They less frequently like typical entertainment programs such as mysteries, comedies, and dance music. These differences remain, furthermore, even when formal education is taken into account.

Similar consistencies on other questions make us confi-

TABLE 19

SELECTED EVENING PROGRAM PREFERENCES
OF PEOPLE CLASSIFIED ACCORDING TO
THEIR INTEREST IN SERIOUS
PROGRAMS*

Favorite Program Types	Listen Mostly for Entertain- ment	Like Both, Now Satisfied	Want More Serious Programs	
Public issues.............	28%	48%	60%	more serious
Classical music...........	20	29	47	than enter-
Semiclassical music.......	25	35	43	taining
Religious.................	15	21	30	
Complete drama..........	40	49	49	
News....................	70	76	77	
Sports...................	33%	35%	33%	
Quiz shows..............	58	59	54	
Hillbilly music...........	29%	27%	20%	more enter-
Mysteries................	44	43	34	taining than
Comedy..................	63	62	51	serious
Dance music.............	57	50	38	

* Greatest differences in favor of serious-mindedness at top of table; greatest differences in favor of entertainment-mindedness at bottom of table.

dent of our main result. Listeners who say that they want more serious programs also read more books, no matter what their educational level. In addition they are older. We noted previously that young people are generally less interested in serious matters. The fact that they make fewer requests for more serious programs is further evidence for the validity of our question.[11]

We might expect the serious listeners to be characterized in other ways. Men, for example, are supposed by tradition to be less interested in frivolous matters and more interested in serious intellectual questions. According to our findings,

[11] The data are reported in Table 18, Appendix C.

however, there is no sex difference in demand for serious programs. For people living in small communities radio is one of the most easily accessible sources of information. Compared with the residents of large cities, they have fewer opportunities to use public libraries, to enroll for adult education courses, to attend lectures or concerts, to have access to specialized journals, and so on. We should expect, therefore, that interest in serious programs would progressively increase as we moved from larger to smaller communities. This is not borne out by the data, however, for we find no consistent relationship between community size and interest in serious programs.

Finally, we tried once more to see whether war experience had made veterans more serious and therefore more interested in serious radio programs. The results are inconclusive, possibly because the number of cases is small. Below twenty-nine, veterans are more likely than nonveterans to say that they want serious programs. In the age group between thirty and thirty-nine, however, the relationship is reversed. We might speculate that the younger veterans were more impressionable and were therefore more influenced by their war experiences, but there is a complicating factor: Veterans, at least those in the present survey, are somewhat better educated, and they come from somewhat higher socio-economic strata. How much of their interest in serious programs is due to these factors, and how much to their war experience, is difficult to determine. It is probably best not to attempt any conclusive answer on the basis of this evidence.

What does it all add up to?

At the time when radio was first developing as a mass medium there was great hope that it would usher in an era of adult education. People who were deprived of educational opportunities in their youth, those who had never acquired too much skill in reading, could now learn just by listening to educational programs. But this hope was never realized. Learning from radio required more motivation and more mental training than had been anticipated. It is true that there were hundreds of thousands of people who listened to serious programs. But everyone had become accustomed to the fact that millions listened to entertainment programs. The result was a general feeling of disappointment and discouragement. It seemed that radio education was not here to stay.

A careful review of the present survey indicates that there are millions of people in this country who want more serious programs. They are people who do listen to the radio and whose formal education indicates that not many other avenues of information are open to them. The market for serious programs seems to be both larger and more important than has been commonly believed in recent years.

In our earlier survey listeners pointed to a wide variety of programs which had "added to their information or knowledge."[12] But even if we interpret the notion of educational radio broadly, it is still likely that programs with more serious content will have lower ratings. Obviously, the mere size of audiences is important in a system of commercial radio. To some extent, there is a real conflict between the cultural responsibilities and the commercial interests of American broadcasters. But the problem need not be put in terms of two mutually exclusive alternatives. It would be foolish to make radio so sophisticated that it loses its audiences, but it would be the failure of a mission not to exploit its cultural possibilities. The best thing for the broadcaster to do is to keep the volume of educational broadcasts slightly above what the masses want. In this way he may contribute to a systematic rise in the general cultural level without defeating the educational goal by driving audiences away. This policy will disappoint some educators and it will alienate some listeners, but it is precisely the kind of compromise solution which must be found.

[12] See Paul Lazarsfeld and Harry Field, *The People Look at Radio*, p. 57. Chapel Hill: The University of North Carolina Press, 1946.

CHAPTER III

THE PEOPLE LOOK AT RADIO

We now have a general picture of the way in which the American listening audience uses radio. But knowing something of listening habits and preferences tells only one side of the story. We must also determine how the audience appraises radio: How does radio compare with other institutions in the community? What features are most likely to evoke criticism? How fair is it? In this chapter we shall present a kind of "score card" for radio, summarizing the way in which it is evaluated by listeners.

It may be well to emphasize once more that such a score card must be looked at cautiously. As we put it in the earlier report:

> How can a social institution, like radio, be truly evaluated as to its present performance? What type or types of yardsticks can be successfully used?
>
> At first glance, it might seem that in a democracy a public opinion survey would not only be a good but also a sufficient measure. But reflection indicates that while opinion surveys are one of the essential tools, they cannot stand alone. At least two other methods for evaluating any institution have to be taken into account.
>
> One obvious approach is to see *whether the product lives up to a high standard*. Whether it be an automobile, a can of soup, or a program schedule, there are measures by which performances can be gauged. These are different for different products. In an automobile, it is efficiency and reliability; in a soup, it is taste and purity. What is it for radio programs? Quite a number of criteria are essential for the adequate evaluation of radio: Are the programs diversified enough to satisfy different groups in the population? How many of them live up to

the aesthetic standards on which experts can agree? How much do they conform to the tastes and values prevailing in the American community? Is there a spirit of experimentation and a drive for self-improvement noticeable in the whole program fare? . . .

Yet, knowing what makes a good program, by objective standards, tells only one side of the story. An institution such as radio has social implications which go beyond its immediate product. There is no doubt, for instance, that generally speaking the more money a broadcaster has to build his program structure, the better the technique and talent of the programs. A most impressive program schedule could probably be arranged by taking the top programs of all the major stations, and developing an "all-star" schedule which could be heard on all radio stations at the same time. But no one would seriously consider such a proposition. The American tradition is to favor divided ownership and regional differentiation. . . . So, a study of the *social structure and social implications of the radio industry* would seem to be a second necessary element in an over-all evaluation.

One could imagine a radio system which reflects the highest social and aesthetic standards but to which no one would listen. While the radio industry is expected to be a creative leader in the community, nobody wants it to lose contact with what the general public approves of and likes. *Approval by public opinion*—acceptance by the ultimate consumer—is as important a criterion of evaluation as program standards and social implications.

If the public's reaction to radio is presented and analyzed in much detail in the following pages, it is done with the conviction that a very important piece of information is contributed. *But it is done also with the full knowledge that public opinion is only one of several pillars upon which the final evaluation of radio should be based.*[1]

Over-all Appraisal

Radio is not a single, isolated experience such as seeing a Broadway play or taking a vacation. It is woven into the

---

[1] Paul Lazarsfeld and Harry Field, *The People Look at Radio*, pp. 3-5. Chapel Hill: The University of North Carolina Press, 1946.

daily pattern of our lives year in and year out. A program that appeals to us today may not please us tomorrow. We may like one program and dislike the next. In one phase of a person's life radio may fill an important function; in another phase it may have no place at all. Still, people may be able to look at it in its entirety and to have a general attitude toward radio as a whole.

As in the previous survey, we tackled the problem of over-all appraisal by asking each respondent:

> In every community the schools, the newspapers, the local government, each has a different job to do. Around here, would you say that the schools are doing an excellent, good, fair, or poor job? How about the newspapers? The radio stations? The local government? The churches?

A question such as this belongs to a group of techniques widely used in social research. If one wants to know how an American feels about Turks or Swedes, a common method is to ask whether he would be willing to room with or to see his sister marry a member of one of these nationalities. If the question is how much children dislike certain chores, they might be asked whether they would prefer to eat worms rather than wash dishes or clean the chicken coop every day. Such attitude questions are never meant to be taken literally.[2] They give the respondent an opportunity to express in a comparative way how he feels about Swedes or dish-washing or radio. Experience has shown that, from the answers to these questions, we can classify people in broad groups varying along a line from a positive to a negative attitude. It is unlikely that many respondents would ever be interested in writing an essay on the kind of job being done by the radio stations or the local governments in their communities. But from their answers to such a question we can tell something of how they feel about radio compared with local government.

---

[2] See Gardner Murphy, Lois Murphy, and Theodore Newcomb, *Experimental Social Psychology*, Chapter XIII. New York: Harper & Brothers, 1937.

This question is revealing in several respects. Table 20 shows that at both times radio came out well in the comparison: In the earlier survey 82 per cent considered radio's over-all performance "excellent" or "good"; now 70 per cent do. Someone might object that the four terms used to rate radio are vague, and that they may not connote the same things for all the people interviewed. That is why a comparison is so important. The comparison shows that in 1945 radio was rated higher than any of the four other institutions; in 1947, only the churches ranked higher.

TABLE 20

OVER-ALL APPRAISAL OF FIVE INSTITUTIONS
(1945 and 1947 compared)

	RADIO		CHURCHES		NEWS-PAPERS		SCHOOLS		LOCAL GOVERN-MENT	
	1945	1947	1945	1947	1945	1947	1945	1947	1945	1947
Excellent.....	28%	14%	25%	22%	12%	9%	17%	13%	7%	4%
Good........	54	56	51	54	56	54	45	46	38	38
Fair.........	10	18	12	13	21	24	18	21	29	31
Poor.........	1	4	2	2	4	5	5	4	9	11
Don't know..	7	8	10	9	7	8	15	16	17	16
	100%	100%	100%	100%	100%	100%	100%	100%	100%	100%

It is interesting to note that, although the respondents were somewhat more critical of all of the institutions about which they were questioned in the present survey, the difference is particularly marked in the case of radio. The proportion of people saying that radio was doing an "excellent" job dropped from 28 per cent in 1945 to 14 per cent in 1947. The proportion saying that radio was doing only a "fair" or "poor" job rose from 11 per cent to 22 per cent.

This lower level of satisfaction is further evidence for the readjustments in communications habits during the post-war era. As we saw in the previous chapter, the American public is becoming less dependent on radio as its primary source of news; its great advantage of immediacy is less important now than it was during the war years. As a result, it is viewed somewhat more critically.

We know from psychological studies that such an appraisal is a complex phenomenon which depends on at least two factors. In the first place there is the attitude toward radio itself: Does the individual like radio basically, is he satisfied with the program fare offered him, does he depend on radio for varied uses, and so on? Secondly, his appraisal depends on his tendency to criticize. There are some individuals who are loth to criticize except when they are extremely irritated; there are others who will find fault with radio, as well as with anything else, at the slightest provocation, or perhaps even without provocation. Two respondents who appraise radio differently need not have different basic attitudes: It may be that one says "good" because he is satisfied with radio and not inclined to criticize, whereas the other says only that radio is doing a "fair" job, because, although he is satisfied, he also tends to find fault.

TABLE 21

APPRAISAL OF RADIO ACCORDING TO AMOUNT
OF EVENING LISTENING
(1947 Survey)

	AMOUNT OF EVENING LISTENING		
	Less Than One Hour	1-3 Hours	3 Hours or More
Appraisal of radio:			
Excellent............	9%	13%	21%
Good...............	54	60	61
Fair................	22	20	14
Poor...............	7	4	2
Don't know.........	8	3	2
	100%	100%	100%

We need not discuss this point only theoretically, for the data in both surveys show how the two factors—basic satisfaction and tendency to criticize—enter into the over-all satisfactions with radio. We find in both surveys that the radio fans are more likely to feel that radio is doing an "excellent" job; this is true even when education is held constant.

At the same time, we find a distinct relationship between what people say about radio and what they say about other institutions. Table 22 classifies the respondents according to their criticism of the other institutions about which they were asked. (A statement that any institution was doing only a "fair" or "poor" job was considered a criticism.) The table then records the way in which radio is appraised by each of these groups.

TABLE 22

APPRAISAL OF RADIO ACCORDING TO CRITICISM OF OTHER INSTITUTIONS
(1947 Survey)

	CRITICAL OF:				
Appraisal of radio:	No Other Inst.	One Other Inst.	Two Other Inst.	Three Other Inst.	Four Other Inst.
Excellent........	16%	17%	10%	6%	3%
Good...........	67	56	49	41	30
Fair............	7	17	28	34	47
Poor...........	2	3	6	10	11
Don't know.....	8	7	7	9	9
	100%	100%	100%	100%	100%

An over-all appraisal such as this is still crude, however. It gives no insight into the sources of dissatisfaction, into the particular features of radio which provoke criticism.

Annoyances and Dissatisfactions

Specific complaints about radio can be approached by two methods, both of which were used in the present survey. In the first place, direct questions can be asked about matters presumed to be sources of criticism. In the second place, "free-answer" questions can be asked which allow the respondents to mention spontaneously whatever it is about radio that annoys them.

The question used to tap spontaneous criticisms in both the earlier and present surveys reads as follows:

Do you ever feel like criticizing when you listen to the radio?

At both times approximately two-thirds of the listeners said that they were sometimes critical while listening to the radio.

In order to make comparisons possible, this question was elaborated in the present survey. In addition to asking about radio, we also asked the respondents if they ever felt like criticizing when they read newspapers or saw a movie. The complete results are reported in Table 23.

TABLE 23

PROPORTION WHO SOMETIMES FEEL LIKE CRITICIZING DIFFERENT MEDIA
(1947 Survey)

Sometimes feel like criticizing:

Radio	67%
Newspapers	68
Movies*	66

---

* Among those individuals who had seen at least one movie during the previous month.

The most striking feature of Table 23 is the constancy of the criticisms. No matter which medium they are asked about, approximately two-thirds of the respondents say that they experience occasional dissatisfaction. This suggests once more the existence of an underlying critical tendency, for it does not seem likely that, without it, we would find such constancy. Just as we found confirmation previously, so we do here too. There is a marked relationship between criticism of each of the media: Critical radio listeners are also critical newspaper readers and critical moviegoers. We can say, in fact, that the critics in each case are almost always the same people.[3]

When we examine the question carefully, we see that it is in the nature of a psychological test. From a logical standpoint, no one should answer "no," for it is unrealistic to suppose that there is any repeated activity, such as radio listening or newspaper reading or movie going, which does not provoke occasional criticism. For this reason, the figures in Table 23 should not be taken too literally; we should not consider them an exact indication of how many people experience occasional dissatisfaction with the different media. We can safely say that *everyone* experiences such annoyance, but that only two-thirds bother to express it. The people who say that they never feel like criticizing radio, newspapers, or movies are relatively unsophisticated: They are less well educated, they read fewer books, and so on.

There is also some indication that respondents are more often critical of the medium on which they are more dependent. Table 24 considers only those respondents who sometimes are critical of either radio or newspapers; it shows that a majority of the individuals who rely on newspapers as their primary source of news criticize newspapers but not radio, whereas a majority of those who depend mainly on radio are occasionally annoyed with radio but never with newspapers.

We may explain this finding in the following way: A

---

[3] See Appendix C, Table 19.

TABLE 24

CRITICISM OF RADIO OR NEWSPAPERS ACCORD-
ING TO PRIMARY SOURCE OF NEWS

	PRIMARY SOURCE OF NEWS	
	Newspapers	*Radio*
Occasionally critical of newspapers, but not of radio..............	58%	48%
Occasionally critical of radio, but not of newspapers.............	42	52
	100%	100%

person who is dependent on one of the media for most of his news makes more demands of that medium; his very reliance makes him expect more and look for more. His occasional criticism, then, is understandable; it is the result of an almost inevitable gap between what he wants from the medium and what it offers him. This kind of sporadic criticism is, of course, quite different from a general feeling that radio is doing a "poor" job; it is an expression of the minor irritations which accompany any repeated activity.[4]

The question was used mainly as a dragnet, deliberately designed to bring out all possible criticism. What clues did it yield; what specific features of radio were mentioned as sources of annoyance?

First and foremost was radio advertising, mentioned by 26 per cent of the listeners. Some respondents criticized the amount of advertising; others the content; still others the

---

[4] In our earlier report, we talked of "lovers' quarrels" with radio, for we found that occasional annoyance became more frequent as amount of listening increased. (See Paul Lazarsfeld and Harry Field, *The People Look at Radio*, p. 10. Chapel Hill: The University of North Carolina Press, 1946.) In the present study, however, there was no relationship between amount of listening and annoyances.

timing and form of presentation. In the following chapter, we shall analyze these attitudes toward radio commercials in greater detail.

An unanticipated result was that mystery and crime programs were singled out for criticism by 15 per cent of the radio audience, a number exceeded in size only by those who criticized commercials. It developed that their complaints were very specific ones. They said, for example, that mystery programs are "bad" or "too exciting" for young children, that "they give publicity on crime and tell you how to commit a murder." They suggested that these programs not be broadcast until "after 9 p.m. when children have gone to bed." In the light of these comments it is not surprising to find that the critics are most frequently married women and housewives.

For a number of reasons this result deserves careful attention. First of all, a critical attitude toward mystery programs seems to be a new development. In the previous survey they were mentioned by so few critics that they were not separated in any special category and are therefore lost among the "miscellaneous" dissatisfactions. Secondly, although 15 per cent may seem a small portion of the radio audience, we must remember that the criticisms were spontaneous ones, not prompted by a direct question on mystery programs. From our general research experience we know that the number of people who volunteer an opinion or criticism is very much smaller than the number uncovered in answer to a direct question. It seems likely, therefore, that if our sample had been asked explicitly about mystery programs, a considerably larger number would have turned out to be critics. Finally, it is interesting to note that, although our adult audience criticizes mystery programs as listening fare for children, they place this program type high on their own list of favorites. There is, of course, a relationship between criticism and selection of mysteries as a preferred program type: Those who volunteer criticisms are less likely to mention crime shows as a favorite. But some of the critics do select mystery shows for their own radio listening. This suggests the possibility that the adult audience calls upon more demanding standards where their children's listening is involved. With only the data which we have at hand, little more can be said about the issue. However, the prominence of the criticisms in our present study suggests an important topic for future researches.

Another group of criticisms, mentioned by 10 per cent, was directed toward news broadcasters and commentators; they were chided for being unfair, for being "Communists," for not always presenting the truth. We shall return to this question of fairness presently.

Finally, 9 per cent of the listeners criticized daytime serials. They were called monotonous, boring, or silly; their numbers were objected to; and their intellectual level was deplored. These criticisms were somewhat more frequent than in the earlier study, where only 4 per cent of the listeners mentioned daytime serials specifically. There has been so much research on daytime listening, and the facts are by now so well established, that we considered it superfluous to explore these criticisms further.[5]

The spontaneous criticisms of radio, then, centered around advertising, mystery programs, news broadcasts, and daytime serials. We anticipated some of these criticisms—those concerned with radio advertising and fairness—and therefore our survey included direct questions on these issues. We turn now to a more detailed examination of these questions.

Fairness

For Americans, "fairness" is a quality which invites high praise; "unfairness" in any activity, whether a sports contest, a political campaign, or a radio program, brings only strong censure.

Another facet of the public's over-all evaluation of radio is their appraisal of its fairness. Do they feel that radio sta-

---

[5] See Paul F. Lazarsfeld and Helen Schneider, "Radio Research in Action," in *Communications Research 1948-49* (edited by Lazarsfeld and Stanton). New York: Harper & Brothers, 1949.

tions present "both sides" of every issue, that they present all the facts of any situation? These are the requirements of fairness in the field of communications.

The question used to determine attitudes on this point, and the answers which it elicited in both surveys, are presented in Table 25.

TABLE 25

"I'd like to ask you how *fair* radio stations and newspapers generally are. For example, do you think radio stations are generally fair in giving both sides of public questions? How about newspapers in general?"

	Per Cent Saying "Fair"	
	1945	*1947*
Radio stations..................	81%	79%
Newspapers....................	39	55

At both times of questioning, the great majority of listeners felt that radio stations were fair in their handling of controversial issues. When one realizes how many listeners would disagree with the individual opinions of various commentators, this fact is impressive.

Table 25 should not be used for invidious comparisons of newspapers and radio. After all, newspapers are entitled, by tradition, to editorial opinion and they do not claim to present both sides of every argument. The present question just shows that, barring further evidence to the contrary, the American public feels that radio is usually fair in its treatment of controversial issues.

A second observation is that, although the judgment of radio's fairness remained virtually constant between our two surveys, newspapers made a large gain in this respect. Previously, only slightly more than one-third of the respondents considered newspapers fair; now, over one-half do. We may speculate for a moment as to the meaning of this change. It may be that the less favorable judgment in the earlier period is due, partially at least, to the fact that for many years before 1945 American newspapers had generally been hostile to the Roosevelt administration, whereas the public had favored it. This disagreement expressed itself in the feeling that newspapers were unfair; and it came to an end with Roosevelt's death in 1945. The more widespread feeling in 1947 that newspapers were fair is probably also a reflection of the more important role which newspapers achieved during the postwar era.

The great majority of listeners consider radio fair. Still there is a minority which is critical in this respect. In the light of previous findings it is no surprise to learn that these critics are more likely to appraise radio less favorably on other questions as well. The relationship between the different evaluation questions is, in fact, a marked one.[6] And, just like the critics of other features of radio, the listeners who consider radio stations unfair are relatively more numerous in the better educated groups.

To some extent a feeling that radio stations are unfair is also associated with relative lack of interest in radio: Light listeners, on all educational levels, find radio more unfair than do heavy listeners.[7] Strictly speaking, our data do not permit us to determine which of these two factors is the cause and which the effect. There can be little doubt from a psychological point of view, however. It is psychologically unrealistic to suppose that light listeners are such because they feel that radio is unfair: There are so many programs in which the question of fairness or unfairness is irrelevant that listeners who wanted to avoid programs they considered unfair could do so and still listen a great deal. It is more probable, therefore, that amount of listening is in some way a "cause" and judgment of fairness an "effect." Or, as seems most likely, the same lack of interest which brings about light

---

[6] Appendix C, Table 20.
[7] Appendix C, Table 21.

listening may also lead to a negative attitude toward radio's fairness.

We might expect that members of the working class would find radio less fair than do professionals or business men. One does occasionally hear that labor unions have difficulties in buying air time, in getting their side of a dispute presented, and so on. Our data indicate, however, that the rank and file members of the working class do not share these critical attitudes to any degree: Even when education is taken into account there are no differences in judgments of radio's fairness either according to socio-economic status or according to occupation.[8]

TABLE 26

RESPONSIBILITY FOR UNFAIRNESS OF RADIO OR NEWSPAPERS

"Who do you think is chiefly responsible for radio's (the newspapers') unfairness—the radio station (newspaper) owner, the commentator or announcer (columnist or reporter) who gives the news, the advertisers who sponsor the news, or someone else?"

Radio			*Newspapers*
Advertisers...............	32%	7%	.........Advertisers
Station owner.............	26	53	.........Newspaper owner
Commentator or			Columnist or
announcer..............	18	16	.... reporter
Someone else.............	12	13	.........Someone else
Don't know..............	12	11	.........Don't know
The 13% saying	100%	100%	The 37% saying
Radio is "Unfair"			Newspapers are
			"Unfair"

---

[8] See Appendix C, Tables 22 and 23. The only conspicuous differences are in the number of "Don't know" answers, and this we can attribute to the lower educational level of the working class as compared with the business and professional classes. These differences disappear when education is controlled.

A new feature of the present survey was an attempt to determine who was blamed for the unfairness of either radio or the newspapers. Individuals who said they thought radio or newspapers unfair were asked the questions reported in Table 26.

The first point to note is the similarity between radio and newspapers on the last three lines of this table. Newspaper columnists and reporters are blamed as frequently as radio commentators and announcers; the miscellaneous personnel collected under the heading "Someone else" share equal responsibility; and the "Don't know" answers are as frequent in the case of radio as they are in the case of newspapers.

It is only when advertisers and owners are considered that we find discrepancies between the two media. Our interviewees hold sponsors and station owners about equally responsible for radio's unfairness. They overwhelmingly blame newspaper owners and publishers for any unfairness which they detect in the press. Or, to put it another way, radio advertisers are blamed more than four times as frequently as newspaper advertisers; station owners are blamed only half as frequently as publishers.

It is interesting to see how certain technical differences between the two media are reflected in this result. In the first place, advertisers do not sponsor columns of news or comment in papers as they do on the radio; their connection with, and influence on, the editorial content of newspapers is perhaps not as apparent therefore. Secondly, we may speculate that newspapers seem to have a greater number of small and diversified advertisers than does radio. It is true, of course, that many commercial announcements are sponsored by local companies, and we have no evidence that listeners are not aware of this fact. But the most popular programs, the "big-name" programs, are often sponsored by large corporations. This may lead to the feeling that radio advertisers are more powerful and influential. Finally, it is easier not to see the advertisements in newspapers than it is not to hear them on the radio, and their number may therefore be underestimated.

All of these factors, inherent in the current systems of operation, make the role of advertisers more noticeable in radio than in the newspapers. The result is that responsibility for unfairness is much more frequently placed at the feet of radio sponsors than is the case with newspaper advertisers.

On the other hand, radio stations are relatively depersonalized institutions, with their alphabetic call-letters, their combination into large networks, and what seems to be the almost intentional avoidance of publicity on the part of station owners. This is in marked contrast to the fame and public notice of such publishers as Hearst, McCormick, Gannett, Knight, and so on. It is quite likely that, if put to the test, more people could name the publishers of newspapers in their communities than could correctly identify the station owners. Furthermore, many newspaper owners are frank to admit that they publish their papers in order to express their opinions and foster the causes which have their support. For reasons such as these, the newspaper publisher is blamed more frequently than the station owner for the unfairness which listeners find in the two media.

Listeners criticized radio's unfairness far less frequently than they did radio advertising. It is in order, then, to ask precisely what they object to in radio commercials, how far-reaching these criticisms are, and what implications they have for the radio industry.

Chapter IV

SOME OBSERVATIONS ON ADVERTISING

The basic questions which we used to study attitudes toward advertising were simple, but quite distinct in their approach. First, we asked the respondents to mention any feature of radio which annoyed them. In this way we could single out those people who criticized advertising with minimum suggestion from the questionnaire. The second question was more direct. We showed the respondents a list of four explicit statements about commercials—ranging from a positive statement of approval to a negative statement that all advertising should be taken off the air—and asked them to select the one which most nearly described their attitudes. In the third question we tried to approximate a fairly concrete situation in which the respondents might be in a position to act according to their feelings about advertising. We reminded them that other countries, like England, support radio, not by advertising revenue, but by listener fees; we asked our respondents whether they would approve such a system, whether they would pay a fee of $5 a year if they could hear radio programs of the present standard without advertising.[1] Finally, we showed the respondents a series of statements about radio commercials and asked them whether they agreed or disagreed with the arguments. We shall return to these statements when we consider specific complaints about radio advertising.

[1] The question of whether or not a fee of $5 would be sufficient to pay for high caliber talent is beside the point here. The question was designed to serve as one approach to attitudes toward advertising, not as a "straw vote" on a concrete plan for subscription radio.

Table 27 shows the proportion of critics revealed by each of our first three questions.

TABLE 27

PROPORTION OF CRITICS OBTAINED BY
THREE QUESTIONS ON ADVERTISING

Voluntary criticism of radio advertising.........	26%
Would pay license fee of $5 a year.............	20
"I don't like advertising on the radio, but I'll put up with it"..............................	22 }31%
"If it were up to me, I'd cut out all advertising on the radio."...............................	9

What might be called marked criticism, then, varies between 20 per cent and 31 per cent, depending on the type of question asked. This parallels very closely the findings of the earlier survey.

These three questions probably represent a fair way of tapping the different elements entering into general attitudes toward advertising. In one query we check whether the respondent's criticism of commercials is foremost in his mind: Does he mention advertising as soon as the idea of criticizing radio is suggested to him? In another question we check whether the respondent is really willing to make a sacrifice for his critical convictions. In the third case, we accept mere verbal statements, but they are worded in a way that is likely to bring out whatever negative attitude does exist.

There is a statistical procedure which makes it possible to combine the answers to three such questions so as to obtain the best estimate of the number of people who have an underlying negative reaction to commercials. This underlying reaction is relatively free from incidental elements which may be involved in answers to single questions. Some people, for instance, may be strongly critical of commercials, but just not have the $5 to pay a fee. Other people, as we have already seen, seem to have negative temperaments which dispose them to criticize commercials just as they criticize everything else. The "latent" attitude eliminates these extraneous elements.[2] Applying the statistical techniques to our data, we found that 26 per cent of the respondents have a basically critical attitude.

Perhaps there is some question as to why the respondents who said that they could "put up with advertising" were included among the critics. The two checklist statements reported in Table 27 were not the only alternatives provided in the question; there were two others from which the respondents could select. The complete checklist question, and the results which it yielded, are shown in Table 28.

TABLE 28

"Which one of these four statements comes closest to what you yourself think about advertising on the radio?"

I'm *in favor* of advertising on the radio...........	32%
I *don't particularly mind* advertising on the radio...	35
I don't like advertising on the radio, but I'll *put up with it*......................................	22
If it were up to me, I'd *cut out* all advertising on the radio......................................	9
Don't know..................................	2
	100%

Superficial analysis of these statements might make some other combinations of answers seem more appropriate. We have little difficulty in classifying the respondents who selected the first or the fourth alternatives. There can be little

---

[2] The statistical techniques through which this latent attitude is determined are briefly described in Appendix E. We shall use them again in a later section of this chapter, when specific complaints about commercials are considered.

doubt that those who say they would like to "cut out" all radio advertising are critics in this respect. There is also little doubt that those who say that they are "in favor" of advertising have a definitely positive attitude.[3]

The meaning of the two remaining statements is not so clear. It is not immediately obvious from their wording whether these alternatives are indicative of a neutral attitude, or whether they are nearer one or the other extreme position. Some readers may feel that we are unfair to the radio broadcasting industry when we include among the critics those respondents who say they will "put up with advertising." Other readers may feel that, on the contrary, we underestimate the number of critics by not including in their ranks the 35 per cent who say they "don't particularly mind" radio advertising.

We decided, however, to place the listeners who said that they could "put up with commercials" in the ranks of critics, and to group together those who said that they didn't "particularly mind" advertising along with those who said explicitly that they were "in favor" of advertising.

This decision was not an arbitrary one, but was based, rather, on a simple statistical procedure. Because of the clarity of the two extreme alternatives, being "in favor" of advertising or wanting to have it all "cut out," we know that the respondents who selected them are the definite partisans and the outspoken critics, respectively. Our first step was to study the answers given by these two unambiguous groups to other questions on advertising. These answers are reported in Table 29.

---

[3] There is a certain amount of ambiguity in the wording of this alternative. The phrase, "in favor of advertising," may be understood as having political implications; that is, respondents may feel that the alternative to being in favor of advertising on the radio is to be in favor of some noncommercial system of broadcasting. As we shall see when further details of attitudes toward commercials are examined, however, there can be little doubt that the listeners who checked this alternative held a definitely positive attitude.

TABLE 29

VOLUNTARY CRITICISMS AND WILLINGNESS TO PAY FEE ACCORDING TO GENERAL ATTITUDE TOWARD ADVERTISING

| | GENERAL ATTITUDE | | | |
	In Favor	Don't Mind	Put up With	Cut Out
Proportion who volunteer criticisms of advertising...	14%	22%	43%	44%
Proportion who would pay license fee of $5 a year.....	5	12	39	61

We note that few of the partisans but nearly half of the critics volunteered spontaneous criticisms of radio advertising; similarly, only a negligible number of partisans but well over half of the critics would be willing to pay a license fee of $5 in order to hear commercial-free radio.

These answers provided a sort of standard against which to study the behavior of the less easily classified respondents. Do the people who say that they "don't particularly mind" advertising align themselves more with the partisans or with the critics? Or do they form a middle group, somewhere in between the two extremes, when their answers to the supplementary questions are considered? How about the respondents who say that they will "put up with" advertising? The answers to these questions will be found in Table 29. When we examine that once more, we see why it is that the people who "don't particularly mind" advertising are considered to have a relatively favorable attitude. On both questions they behave considerably more like the partisans than like the critics. In their voluntary criticisms of advertising they differ from the partisans by only 8 per cent but they differ from the outspoken critics by 22 per cent. Similarly, in their willingness to pay a license fee they differ from the partisans by 7 per cent and from the critics by fully 49 per cent.

Table 29 also shows why the respondents who "put up with" radio advertising are included in the critical group. By the same sort of procedure employed in the previous paragraphs we find that they behave very much more like the unambiguous critics than like the unambiguous partisans. For example, they differ from the outspoken critics by only 1 per cent when we examine the frequency with which they offered spontaneous criticisms of advertising, but they differ from the partisans by 29 per cent in this respect. Again, they differ from the partisans by 34 per cent but from the critics by only 22 per cent when we consider their willingness to pay a license fee.

One interesting point to note is that the respondents who "put up with" advertising are more hostile to commercials when it does not cost them anything. They volunteer criticisms of advertising just as frequently as do the unambiguous critics. But when they are called on to make a sacrifice for their convictions, when they are asked whether they would pay a fee of $5 in order to hear radio without commercials, their critical tendencies become considerably less marked— they differ from the critics by a wider margin.

Summarizing the analysis thus far, we can say that somewhat less than one-third of the listeners hold a negative attitude toward radio advertising. Among the remaining two-thirds are 32 per cent who explicitly favor commercials and a final 35 per cent who indicate in various ways that their attitude toward advertising is a not unfriendly one.

What's Wrong with Commercials

It is not enough to know how many people like or dislike advertising. The policy-maker can act only if he also knows what it is specifically that people dislike; he will be served still better if he can attach weights to the various arguments which are brought up. It is not easy to provide such information. The following paragraphs will summarize the efforts which were made in the course of this study.

In the earlier survey we had to start from scratch. Each respondent was asked to tell what it was he objected to in commercials, if he objected at all. The answers were carefully examined and finally were classified in the following five major categories:

> Volume and position
> Uninteresting content
> Overselling
> Violation of taboos
> Attention-getting devices

When the respondents expressed themselves clearly, we could argue fairly convincingly that their criticisms fell in one or another of these five categories. Although they seemed psychologically satisfactory, however, they could not be used for statistical purposes. It was not possible to say which of these five criticisms was most frequent, let alone most important, for many of the comments were so ambiguous that they could not be placed in any one of the five groups. This was especially true of statements that commercials are "too long" or that there are "too many" of them. Such comments are not particularly meaningful, for a listener will not find commercials either too long or too numerous unless he has more specific complaints. He may feel that they are too long because he finds their content uninteresting; or he may think that there are too many commercials because he dislikes attention-getting devices. But general criticisms of length and number reveal little about specific attitudes toward commercials.

This classification scheme enabled us to approach the problem more precisely in the present study. Five arguments were developed, one corresponding to each of the five points above.

"Commercials spoil the program by interrupting it."
"Commercials are boring and repetitious."
"Commercials claim too much for the product."
"Commercials are often in bad taste."
"Commercials are noisy and distracting."

On each of these points the respondents were given an opportunity to say that they agreed or disagreed, or that they didn't know.

Before the present study got under way, we conducted a pretest to make sure that these five arguments were understood in the way that they were meant to be. The list of statements was shown to a nation-wide sample of 300 individuals, and whenever a respondent expressed agreement with any one of them, he was asked to give an example or to elaborate in more detail what he meant by that agreement. The comments obtained in this way were very similar to those we had studied in 1945. In other words, on the basis of his comments alone we would have classified the respondent in the same way that he classified himself by his responses to each of the five statements.

The new procedure, however, has one great advantage. It enables us to state how frequent each of the criticisms actually is. Before turning to this point, a word of warning is in order. The reader will notice that all five statements are worded negatively: Agreement with any one of them means criticism of commercials. Psychologists have discovered that there is a tendency for individuals to agree rather than disagree with any given statement. If our statements had been phrased in terms complimentary to radio commercials, all of the respondents who *dis*agreed with the negative form would have agreed with the positive form. But there can be no doubt that, because of this psychological tendency, some people who agreed with the negative form would also have agreed with the positive formulation. In later pages we shall present some inferential evidence on this point. For the time being it is enough for the reader to recognize that, because of the way in which the statements were worded, the absolute amount of criticism is somewhat exaggerated. This need not concern us at the moment, however, for we are interested only in the relative amount of criticism obtained for each of the statements.

Table 24 in Appendix C details the proportions of agreements and disagreements on each of the five items. We find that there were three criticisms agreed to by a majority of the respondents: 60 per cent said that commercials spoil a program by interrupting it and that they claim too much for the product; 58 per cent said that they are boring and repetitious. A smaller number of respondents, 46 per cent, agreed that commercials are often in bad taste, or that they are noisy and distracting.

These results are corroborated by further data and observations. First of all, it is easy to explain why two of the criticisms are relatively less frequent. Both of them are objections raised by fairly special subgroups in the listening audience. The argument that radio advertising is noisy, for example, is an objection confined in the main to critics of singing commercials; we know this from the comments obtained in our earlier study and in our pretest of the present survey. But, as we see in Table 30, the critics of singing commercials are only slightly more numerous than their

---

TABLE 30

"How do you feel about singing commercials? In general, do you like them better than straight commercials, or not as well?"

Prefer singing commercials......................	37%
Prefer straight commercials......................	43
No difference....................................	18
Don't know......................................	2
	100%

partisans.[4] As a result, the argument that commercials are noisy and distracting is agreed to by only a part of the total listening audience.

The fact that there are relatively fewer agreements with the statement that commercials are in bad taste can be ex-explained in a similar way. Again we find our clue in the comments obtained from the pretest: When asked to explain what struck them as being in bad taste, many of the listeners who had agreed with this argument mentioned advertisements of beer, wine, and cigarettes. Of course, some listeners find commercials in bad taste for other than moral reasons. But moral objections appeared quite frequently in connection with this argument, and, since they are confined to a part of the total radio audience, perhaps those living outside metropolitan areas and older women everywhere, the criticism is not so widespread as others.

The remaining three arguments require most serious consideration. Two of them refer to the content of commercials. First of all, people dislike what is known to the trade as "hard selling." It may be that such techniques lead to increased sales, but there can be little doubt that they also create hostility in the audience. Listeners feel disturbed, and also irked, when claims which they consider extravagant are made for many products. Because of this, the merits of such overselling should be carefully studied. The occasional advantages for the individual advertiser must be weighed against the disadvantages for the broadcasting industry as a whole.

We know also that commercials need not be "boring or repetitious," for in the earlier survey almost every respondent was able to mention a commercial which he liked especially. These were usually characterized by their informative value, by the fact that they were well integrated into the program, or by some entertaining and original feature. Undoubtedly, talent capable of writing such commercials is relatively rare

---

[4] There are a number of interesting observations on the kinds of people who prefer singing commercials. These are reported in Appendix F.

and therefore expensive. But our data indicate that the advertiser would benefit from any efforts made to find and develop this talent. Creative copywriting could do much to overcome negative attitudes toward commercials and might therefore improve the public relations of the whole industry.

Finally, listeners dislike interruptions in radio programs. This is so well-known by now that it hardly deserves comment. But again the broadcaster faces an apparent dilemma. Obviously the coverage is greatest when listeners are caught by surprise in the middle of a program to which they are tuned; it is probably true that commercial messages at the beginning and end of programs leave fewer so-called "impressions." Once more, however, the advantages must be weighed against the disadvantages: Greater coverage must be balanced against the general resistance created by middle commercials. The merits in this case are most difficult for an outsider to judge. One can be pretty certain that overclaiming is not necessary, and that many commercials could be better written than they are now. But how great is the sales advantage of the middle commercial? There is probably no one who really knows. On this point the present study just indicates the need for further investigations, using experimental techniques rather than a survey approach.

Severity of Criticism

So far we have talked only about the frequency of various kinds of criticism, but critical statements can differ also in their *severity*. Sometimes it is possible to see this in the very wording of our statements. If we say that Mr. A. embezzled company funds, it is plain that our accusation is more severe than if we reproach him for eating peas with a knife. But we cannot always infer the relative severity of two critical statements from their wording alone. Which is the more severe criticism—that commercials are boring or that they are noisy?

Fortunately, it was possible to clarify this question of severity in the present case. A severe criticism is one that is likely to be endorsed by respondents who particularly dislike commercials. A severe criticism is also one that is associated with many other critical statements.

In order to study the severity of the five arguments about commercials, we need some measure of the respondents' underlying general attitudes toward radio advertising. This measure is provided by a statistical procedure which is described briefly in Appendix E. Applying it to our data, it was possible to demonstrate that the five arguments form a unit. (In technical jargon we say that they represent a "one-dimensional psychological continuum.") A listener who endorses three or four of the critical statements is more negative in his attitude toward commercials than one who agrees with only one or two statements. And a criticism endorsed by the more hostile listeners is a severe one.

Without going into further details, the results of this statistical analysis can be presented in graphic form. Visualize a kind of thermometer: At the zero point are those statements which involve no criticism; at the 100 per cent point are those which would be endorsed only by the most extreme and violent critics of radio advertising. Each of our five items can be given a position on this scale. This has been done in Graph II. It develops that the criticism that commercials are noisy is most severe, and the objection that they claim too much is least so. The other criticisms fall in between.

This finding underlines the importance of distinguishing between the frequency and severity of complaints. We saw previously that the criticism of noisiness was relatively infrequent. But the listener who does raise this objection has a thoroughly negative attitude toward commercials.

It is in order to ask which one, frequency or severity, should receive priority in the attention of the policy-maker. Obviously the complaints which deserve most serious attention are those which are both frequent and serious. If a decision must be made between seriousness and frequency, it might be wiser for the advertiser to attend first to the more frequent complaints. Severe criticisms are those put forward by the real "enemies" of radio advertising. If one of their complaints is met by the radio industry, it is likely that they will replace it with another complaint. Frequent criticisms, on the other hand, are those endorsed by the largest number of people, and if one of these is remedied, it is probable that the number of radio critics will decrease.

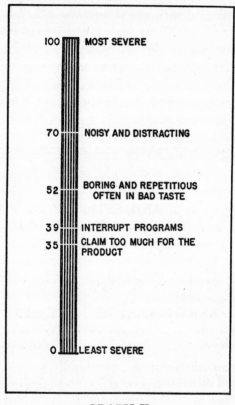

GRAPH II

Severity scores of five statements about
commercials.

Our suggestion that the most frequent criticism should be attended to first is still not specific enough, for, as we recall, three of the five critical statements were endorsed by equal numbers of respondents. Approximately 60 per cent of the listeners agreed that commercials are "boring and repetitious," that they "spoil the program by interrupting it," and that they "claim too much." We therefore need a second criterion to differentiate between the equally frequent objections. This is provided by the severity scores of the various items. By considering simultaneously the frequency and severity of the five complaints, the priority of different courses of remedial action will become clarified. Referring once more to Graph II we find that the most severe of the frequent criticisms is the objection that commercials are "boring and repetitious." Whatever improvements are undertaken might be directed first toward making radio advertising more interesting and varied. The order in which the other criticisms might be attended to is suggested in Table 31.

TABLE 31

FREQUENCY AND SEVERITY OF FIVE
STATEMENTS ABOUT RADIO
COMMERCIALS

	Severity Score
More frequent criticisms:	
Boring and repetitious......................	.52
Interruptions...............................	.39
Strong claims..............................	.35
Less frequent criticisms:	
Noisy and distracting......................	.70
Bad taste..................................	.52

One point in our previous discussion remains to be considered. We indicated that the absolute numbers of respondents endorsing negative statements should not be taken seriously. Only the relative position of a statement when its frequency and severity are considered simultaneously is of any real interest. Although this is almost a matter of common sense, we wanted some evidence. As a check we included three statements which were complimentary to radio commercials. Indeed, these do yield many fewer critics than do comparable statements which are negatively worded. Thirty-two per cent of the listeners *dis*agreed with the positively worded statement that "commercials are often amusing and entertaining"; but when the same issue was approached through a negatively worded statement, 58 per cent agreed that "commercials are boring and repetitious." In other words, a third of the audience was critical when the statement was phrased positively; well over half were critical when a similar argument was put in negative terms. Table 24 in Appendix C indicates that the number of the critics varies by about 25 per cent, depending upon the way in which the statement is worded.

Our primary purpose in including these three check statements was to warn against naive interpretations of absolute frequencies. It might be pointed out, just for the record, that 74 per cent of the respondents agree that "commercials give useful information" about things they may want to buy; 65 per cent say they are "worth-while because they tell you who pays for the program"; 65 per cent find them "often amusing and entertaining." It is interesting to note that the informative value of commercials tops this list. Copywriters might take this as a hint.

The eight statements can be put to still another use. They provided each respondent with eight separate opportunities to express a critical attitude toward radio commercials. It is a simple matter to determine whether the listener was critical at every opportunity, whether he expressed an unfavorable attitude on no items, on one, or two, and so forth. This results in an index which has much to recommend it. In the first place, it is flexible. The nine different score values (no criticisms to eight criticisms) can be combined in many different ways, depending on the particular requirements of our analysis. We can single out those who are never critical and see how they differ from other respondents. We can isolate those who express their distaste for commercials at every opportunity and examine their attitudes on other issues. Or we can combine the different scores in such a way that we obtain a specified distribution of attitude. The classification scheme which most nearly reproduces the distribution of opinion revealed by other advertising questions is shown in Table 32.

TABLE 32

A CRITICISM SCORE

	Number of Unfavorable Reactions	Proportion of Respondents
Level I (+).................	0–1	26%
Level II....................	2–5	50
Level III (−)...............	6–8	24
		100%

This threefold classification of listeners will hereafter be referred to as the "criticism score."

A second advantage of the index is its ability to discriminate between respondents. It is a well-known fact in research that no single question enables us to gauge attitudes and preferences very effectively. Whenever possible, we try to use a complex of questions which cover varied aspects of whatever it is we are studying. The criticism score does just that. It enables listeners who dislike everything about commercials to express their consistent distaste. It permits those who like some features but dislike others to render a split decision.

The criticism score will be used in later sections of this report when we return to consider further aspects of attitudes toward commercials; but, first, a general comment is in order.

The distribution of opinion on radio advertising has been so carefully established in the present survey and it parallels so closely the results of our earlier study that it might be a good idea to consider the matter closed for the time being. Instead of repeatedly counting the critics and partisans, the radio industry might do better to turn its attention to new, and perhaps more important, issues.[5]

There are a number of crucial problems which remain to be studied systematically. Perhaps one of the most important concerns the way in which attitudes develop and the way in which they can be changed. Descriptive information on the number of people who hold one or another attitude is, of course, valuable. But it cannot be put to any very effective use unless we also know what determines the attitudes and how they can be modified. It is not easy to answer these questions. Studies specifically designed to provide answers are expensive in both time and money, and surveys of the present type run into theoretical limitations. It so happens that we can illustrate these difficulties with an example from our investigation.

The Hucksters: Exposure and Attitudes

The publication of Frederic Wakeman's novel and its subsequent production as a motion picture encouraged us to attempt a study of effects in the present survey: We wanted to see how a single document such as this one might affect attitudes toward radio, and especially toward radio advertising.

Although one can debate the literary merits of Wakeman's novel as well as its accuracy in portraying the advertising industry, there can be little doubt as to the author's intentions. He tells, with biting satire, the "inside story"

---

[5] It would be important, of course, to re-examine the distribution of opinion after several years had elapsed in order to see whether any changes had occurred.

of radio advertising: Commercials are the product of low taste, a low estimate of the public's intelligence, and the monotonous application of time-worn tricks.

In order to study the responses to such satire, we included two questions in the present survey, one asking the respondent whether he had read the novel, the other asking whether he had seen the movie. Although study of effects always has great theoretical interest, it is important in this case to place the problem in its proper context. *The Hucksters* could have had only a minor influence on the population as a whole, for only a small proportion either read the book or saw the movie. The exact figures are shown in Table 33.

TABLE 33

EXPOSURE TO *THE HUCKSTERS*

Read the novel.................................. 13%
Saw the movie.................................. 19%

Included among the readers and the moviegoers are 5 per cent of our total sample who both read the book and saw the movie. There is, in fact, a marked relationship: Those who read the book were more likely than the nonreaders to see the movie, and, conversely, those who saw the movie were more likely than the non-moviegoers to read the book. This is some evidence for the "double exposure" we talked of in Chapter I, the fact that people seem to enjoy reading the novels on which a movie they have seen was based, or seeing the movie taken from a book they had read.[6]

We were not surprised to find that educated people read *The Hucksters* more frequently than did less educated respondents. Their greater book consumption makes it likely

---

[6] See pp. 8, 9.

that more of them will have read any particular book which is mentioned. We therefore carried our analysis one step further; we separated the people who had read no books in the previous month from those who had read one, two, or three, and so on; and then, in each group, we studied the original relationship between education and readership of Wakeman's novel.[7] The results of this analysis indicate that there is indeed something more to the relationship than the mere fact that educated people read more, for it turns out that, even with amount of book reading held constant, there is a marked educational difference in reading *The Hucksters*. This novel seems to have a special appeal for better educated groups; or to put it another way, education acts as a sort of predisposition in reading the novel. The same result is found in connection with seeing the movie of *The Hucksters;* even when amount of movie attendance is held constant, the educated people report more frequently that they saw this particular film.[8]

It is likely that *The Hucksters* had two different kinds of effects: It probably changed the attitudes of some people; it probably reinforced the attitudes of others. Because the design of the present study does not permit us to distinguish these two kinds of influences, we shall be cautious in the discussion that follows. In order to avoid all confusion, we shall not use the word "effect" but shall talk only of relationships between exposure and attitudes.

In connection with what sorts of questions do we find differences between those who read the book or saw the movie, and those who did neither?

Because Wakeman's novel dealt almost exclusively with radio advertising, we should expect to find a relationship between exposure and attitudes toward commercials. This, in fact, is the case. As we see in Table 34, those who were exposed to Wakeman's satire on radio advertising are con-

[7] See Appendix C, Table 25.
[8] See Appendix C, Table 26.

siderably more critical of commercials, even when education is held constant.

TABLE 34

PROPORTIONS WITH HIGHEST CRITICISM
SCORE* ACCORDING TO EXPOSURE
TO *THE HUCKSTERS*
AND EDUCATION**

	Per Cent with Highest Criticism Score	
	College	*High School*
Read *The Hucksters*.............	49%	35%
Did not read it.................	35	23
Saw *The Hucksters*.............	48	31
Did not see it....................	36	23

---

* The higher the criticism score, the more negative the attitude toward commercials.

** The reader will note that respondents with only grade school education have not been included in our analysis. So few of them had either read *The Hucksters* or seen the movie that it was impossible to study their attitudes toward radio commercials in relation to their exposure.

We thus find that people who read or saw *The Hucksters* are more critical of radio advertising. This is not what statisticians call a "spurious relationship"—it is not explained by the fact that educated people are more critical and at the same time more likely to expose themselves to *The Hucksters*. For, when the respondents are separated into different educational groups, we still find that exposure and attitude are related. This relationship undoubtedly comes about in a variety of ways: Some people were made more critical by seeing or reading *The Hucksters*; others exposed themselves just because they were more critical.

Our analysis must stop here; but the results are by no means uninteresting. In other fields, too, this mutual interaction between exposure and attitude has been found to be the psychological mechanism by which modern mass media affect the thinking of the population. Even when people elect to read certain books or see certain films which agree with their previously existing attitudes, they are not completely unaffected by that exposure. There is an effect of "reinforcement." The critic who reads *The Hucksters* does not become a critic as a result of this experience, but he most probably becomes more critical. He finds new arguments to bolster his position; he finds new criticisms which he had not thought of before; and so on. In other words, his criticism is strengthened and reinforced by his exposure. [9]

Exposure to *The Hucksters* is not related to any other attitudes. On the question of the kind of job being done by radio, we find only minor and erratic differences between the exposed and unexposed groups on all educational levels. This is not difficult to understand, for neither the novel nor the film dealt specifically with radio's general performance. Wakeman was concerned only with the performance of radio advertisers. Nor are the exposed people more anxious to see radio advertising regulated in some way. There were no differences on this question [10] between those who had read the book and those who had not, or between those who saw the movie and those who did not. This may seem somewhat surprising, since, if exposure is related to a more critical attitude toward commercials, we should expect it to be related to opinions on the regulation of these commercials as well. Attitudes toward "regulation" or "control" are part of a larger and more general complex of attitudes concerning social issues, and they are not easily swayed even when atti-

---

[9] This effect of reinforcement has been studied in various situations, but perhaps the most complete analysis will be found in Lazarsfeld, Berelson, and Gaudet, *The People's Choice.* New York: Columbia University Press, 1948, second edition.

[10] The question to which we refer read as follows: "Do you think that somebody—either the Federal government or the radio industry itself—should see to it that not too much advertising is broadcast on the radio?"

tudes toward the thing to be regulated are changed or strengthened.

This finding serves as a good introduction to the listeners' social attitudes, and their implications for the radio industry as a whole.

Chapter V

TOWARD AN EVER BETTER RADIO

When one plans a study like the present one, one is impressed, indeed overwhelmed, by the number of topics which could be profitably investigated. There is almost no end to the questions on which we should like to have information, and yet, there are very definite limitations to the number that can be answered in any one survey. When the present study was first being discussed, we knew that the Federal Communications Commission would soon start hearings to determine whether radio stations should be permitted to editorialize as newspapers do. It would be interesting to know what listeners thought about this matter. Accordingly, we experimented with a few relevant questions during the preliminary phases of our investigation. It soon developed that, because of the complexity of the issue, nothing less than a complete survey on this one point could have yielded reliable information. Or, consider the fact that broadcasters are gradually beginning to discuss problems of social pathology. Until very recently radio has shied away from these topics, but not so long ago there was an hour-long documentary program, the first of its kind, dealing with problems of venereal disease. Again we might wonder how listeners feel about this: Do they think that broadcasters should be more, or less, outspoken on such subjects? Again it is obvious that no valid answer would be forthcoming from just one or two questions.

A thorough evaluation of radio is really a task for continuing research. New problems should be brought under scrutiny every year. As the scope of these issues enlarges, new tools of investigation will have to be employed. Content analyses, for example, will find much wider use than they have thus far. We might mention one or two problems to which such techniques could be applied. During the war, radio made a sizable contribution to civilian morale by telling listeners how they could help the national defense effort. Woven into the scripts of programs with large audiences was information on the need for blood donors, for air-raid wardens, for the success of war bond drives, and the like. Immediately following the war there was much discussion of continuing these practices in peacetime. It was felt that, by skillful insertions in popular programs, radio could do much to explain the complexity of some contemporary problems and to emphasize the need for participation in worthy causes. But how far have such plans been carried out? How much information on timely social issues is included in entertainment programs? Only a periodic content analysis could provide an answer.

The same techniques could also be used to determine whether the artistic level of average American programs is slowly rising, whether new program ideas are being introduced, whether new types of programs are finding their way onto the air-waves.

We can hope that as time goes on it will become increasingly clear that continuing social research is one of the responsibilities incumbent upon the large communications media. As a matter of fact, it is to the credit of the radio broadcasting industry that it has led the other media of mass communication in showing what can be done.

Yet the policy-maker cannot wait until all the data are in; he must make decisions even though appropriate researches may be lacking. The research student, on his part, has the responsibility of showing the implications of his data, however fragmentary they may be at any given moment. In this last chapter, we shall try to point out some conclusions implied in the findings of the present survey. We shall be able to deal with three topics. The first of these, to which we now turn, concerns the weight to be given criticisms unearthed in the two preceding chapters.

Who Are The Critics?

There is no doubt that the radio broadcasting industry will be pleased with the report card which it receives from its listeners. It will be particularly pleased that at no point do the critics exceed a third of the population. But this minority is a special one, and it therefore deserves special attention.

In the 1945 study we produced a summary table which showed that the critics were drawn mainly from the better educated groups; [1] exactly the same result was found in the present survey. As we can see in Table 35, there is no issue

TABLE 35

PROPORTION WHO ARE CRITICAL OF RADIO ON DIFFERENT EDUCATIONAL LEVELS

	College	High School	Grade School
Proportion who feel that radio is doing a fair or poor job........	31%	23%	18%
Proportion who feel that radio is unfair......................	20	13	11
Proportion who sometimes feel like criticizing radio, for any reason..	79	70	55
Proportion who "put up with" radio advertising or would like it cut off air...................	43	30	26
Proportion who have highest criticism score*...................	40	25	14

* The higher the criticism score, the more critical the attitude toward radio advertising.

[1] See Paul Lazarsfeld and Harry Field, *The People Look at Radio*, p. 67. Chapel Hill: The University of North Carolina Press, 1946.

on which the listeners with grade school education approach the critical attitude of the college-educated listeners.

The conclusions which we drew from this result in 1945 are still as relevant as ever. At the 1946 convention of the National Association of Broadcasters, the senior author of this report was given an opportunity to discuss the findings of the first study. The presentation was centered around a description of these critics, their motivation, and their role in the community. We can do no better today than to quote several paragraphs from that presentation as they were printed in the Information Bulletin of the National Association of Broadcasters:

"Some of you have asked: Isn't the public's great satisfaction with radio the outstanding result of the study? Why then give the critics such conspicuous billing? My most important task today, probably, is to explain this decision and to get you to agree with the reasoning behind it.

"As we progressively discovered who these critics were, we became more and more impressed by them. The dissenting voices come from very desirable groups in the community. They are solid citizens, the well educated men and women, able to express themselves clearly and likely to influence others. This fact brings us to the heart of the problem. The critics are a minority, but obviously a very important one. Why are they your opponents?

"These people are in the stream of the best American tradition. You are all justly proud of the high standard of living which this country has achieved. Having come here as an immigrant, I probably appreciate even more than some of you how much this country has to offer. But no one should think that wages and salaries alone make up a standard of living. If people have no time for their personal pursuits, their incomes do them no good. If they don't have a considerable amount of education, they are unable to enjoy the fine things in American life. The American standard of living is as high as it is because the average citizen here has more money, more leisure time, and a higher level of education than the people of any other country.

"American technology has provided the income. But it is the critics—the great line of American reformers—who have fought for generations to establish schools, to abolish child labor, to reduce working hours. Yet this still does not explain why it is just such people to whom we all owe so much, that it is just these who are so often the critics of radio.

"When I was a high school boy, I saved my allowance for many months to buy a trinket for a girl. She loved it—and in order to display her new possession, she immediately went out with another boy. Can you understand that some of the social innovators feel the way I did at the time of this incident? They have fought for several generations to give people three more hours of free time each day. Now that their old battle is won, they find that people spend this time listening to your radio programs. The intelligent reformer does not begrudge them the fun, nor you the audience. But he hopes that now you in turn will make your contribution to the further development of our standard of living.

"It has been said that radio, like all other modern media of mass communication, plays a triple role today: As a craft, as a business, and as a social force. Your critics admire your craftsmanship; they are sure that you are good businessmen. When they think of radio as a social force, they keep their fingers crossed. No doubt these reformers are often difficult to get along with and because they listen less to the radio, they seem negligible as an audience. But don't be deceived. Even if there are only a few in some of your communities, taken together they are a formidable public force and have won many battles. You and your critics will somehow have to come to terms—for the good of the country, as well as for your own peace of mind."

Undoubtedly the industry is aware of this problem, to some extent at least. Efforts to develop a good code, cooperation with civic organizations, the very fact of the present study, all of these are testimony to the efforts which the industry has made to understand and meet competent criticism, even when it comes only from a minority in the community.

The results of Table 35 deserve equally close study by the critics themselves. Otherwise they are likely to fall into a fallacy of social acoustics. There is a story of a Park Avenue matron who was heard to remark after the 1944 Presidential elections that she was suspicious of the results, because for three months before the election she had talked to no one who intended to vote Democratic. Critics of radio commit the same mistake when they say, as they occasionally do, that "everybody hates commercials" or that "nobody thinks radio is doing a good job." Even the most cursory study of Table 35 will show them how wrong they are. They only deceive themselves and weaken their criticisms when they claim that the majority of listeners hold the same attitudes that they do.

There is one psychological difficulty in the relationship between the critic and the broadcaster which deserves special mention. Criticism of radio derives from basic social forces. It is not directed toward an individual broadcaster and it should never be taken as a personal offense. Furthermore, this criticism is and must be unremitting. Many a broadcaster feels that he is already doing his best; he becomes confused and bewildered by unending prods from the critics. Actually, the social function of criticism is to make sure that the radio man *continues* to do his best. Daily life in America would be much more monotonous if people did not have radios. But radio would be much more monotonous if broadcasters did not have their critics.

Yet, if personal irritations can be eliminated, the critic and the broadcaster will find it fairly easy to get along and to work out policies acceptable to both. For most of the critics in this country have one outstanding characteristic. They do not want to send the sheriff after the broadcaster, nor do they want to "take over" the industry. Most of them want to see their criticisms met within the present framework of the industry. This is the second point to be considered here.

Who Shall Do The Job?

It is a commonplace to point out how complex our social system has become in the last century. It is also a commonplace to say that technological developments are responsible for this complexity. Automobiles cannot be mass-produced by craftsmen working individually in their shops. As a result we find large industrial corporations, which wield economic power of a sort which has widespread repercussions in the society as a whole. This in turn means that the functions of government are modified. No modern state can remain aloof from the economic field, for one of its tasks is to make certain that the giant corporations do not act in any way which would harm public interest. But how far can the state go without impairing basic individual freedoms? What is the right balance between collective social planning and personal liberty? This is perhaps the central problem of our times.

Large-scale organizations are also necessary for the media of mass communication; radio could hardly operate without networks. The matter is still more complicated in the communications field; the magazine industry, the radio industry, newspapers, all are businesses as well as cultural agents for the nation. The traditional controls for business cannot be applied easily to cultural activities. Ideas, we feel, should be left to free competition in the hope that only the best will survive. Even this free competition has changed substantially in recent history, however. One hundred years ago a man who felt that he had been offended by a newspaper publisher could settle the matter in a duel. Today no one who is attacked on the radio would think of challenging the station manager. He asks for time to air his counter-attack and he points to a decision of the FCC which entitles him to this time. The parents' organization which disapproves of some kind of children's program will not deal with two thousand stations individually. Instead, it will try to get the radio industry as a whole to introduce desired provisions into its code, and these provisions would be binding for all stations at once.

Today when these questions of policy arise, they are dealt with through the pressures which various groups bring to bear on other groups. On such matters it is rare indeed that one person will try to influence another directly. But again there are basic problems to be solved. Should the citizens' groups deal with the communications industry directly or with the government as an intermediary?

One must recognize the generality of this problem and not be confused by irrelevant details. Some parents' organizations disapprove of comic books. It so happens that there is no federal comic book commission to which these organizations can turn. But there is no reason why comic books or slick magazines or movies should present a different problem than radio. For the two questions raised by the community in connection with radio are equally applicable to other mass media: To what extent should the individual owner of a radio station or magazine or newspaper be subject to some kind of social control? And, who should exercise this influence?

There is no one who could give definitive answers to these questions, possibly because no such answers exist. But we must act somehow, and to act wisely we must use all the cues that we can find. One cue is the feelings of the population as a whole on these questions.

These considerations led us to include several relevant queries in our survey. We selected a number of issues which previous studies had revealed as being matters of considerable concern to the population. On each of these topics the respondents were asked whether they felt that some kind of obligation should be imposed upon the broadcasters, and, if so, who should see to it that the right policies were pursued. Our approach can best be seen in Table 36. There the wording of the question, the issues involved, and the distribution of answers are presented together.

TABLE 36

"Do you think somebody—either the Federal government or the radio industry itself—should see to it that . . ." (*each item below*)

FOR EACH ITEM ANSWERED "YES": "Who do you think should do that—the Federal government, or the radio industry itself?"

	Nobody	Gov't	Radio	Don't Know	Total
Not too much advertising is broadcast on the radio?	22%	13%	54%	11% =	100%
The profits of radio stations aren't too high?	24	27	28	21 =	100
Radio stations regularly carry programs giving both sides of public issues?	7	23	58	12 =	100
Each station broadcasts a certain number of educational programs?	10	21	57	12 =	100
Radio news broadcasts are accurate?	7	30	52	11 =	100

There were two parts to the question. The first step corresponds to our first problem: To what extent should there be any kind of social control? By and large people feel that there should be some. On none of these five topics did more than one-quarter of the population say that "Nobody" should exercise any kind of regulation. This can be seen in the first column of the table.

The frequency with which some kind of control is called for is an indication of the degree to which people are concerned with these issues. All of these are topics on which the population feels strongly. We can easily visualize other questions on which there would be less frequent demands for some kind of control. For example, there are probably few listeners who care one way or another whether radio stations are owned by banks or newspapers or department stores. Therefore, if we asked our respondents a question on the ownership of stations, we would undoubtedly find fewer of them asking for regulation of any sort. On the other hand, we can as easily visualize other issues on which an even larger number of respondents would favor controls. For instance, no one would like to hear four or five stations broadcasting over the same wave-lengths. If they were asked about it, the respondents would probably agree that the allocation of wave-lengths should be regulated.

Even though the five issues on which we questioned the respondents were all matters of considerable concern, there is marked variation between them. On three of them over 90 per cent of the listeners favor some kind of control; on the remaining two three-quarters do. If we examine the statements closely, we see that they fall into two groups. The two issues on which relatively less concern was expressed dealt with the economics of broadcasting—the issues of radio advertising and radio profits. There were two other issues with definite moral overtones—the accuracy of news broadcasts and the fairness of radio programs. It is in connection with these that the strongest demands for regulation were voiced. We may speculate for a moment as to why this is the case. Our explanation may lie in the fact that Americans have always been concerned with moral issues. This has evidenced itself in the emphasis placed on honesty and fairness, in sympathy for the underdog and a desire to protect him from exploitation, in a dislike for "deals" of any kind, and in similar ways. This great concern has expressed itself further in a willingness, even a desire, to see that moral codes are not violated, and that, if they are, there is some sort of punishment. Economic matters, on the other hand, have been guided by another set of principles. Success was the ultimate criterion, and success seemed most probable under a policy of *laissez-faire*. Accordingly, there is a less widespread desire to see economic matters regulated. It is interesting to note, finally, that by their responses listeners place the supply of educational broadcasts among the "moral" issues.

As we have already indicated, there was a second step in our questioning procedure. The listeners who called for regulation on any one of these five issues were then asked by whom the controls should be imposed. Actually, they were given only two alternatives to choose from: The federal government and the radio industry itself. In future studies one might extend these alternatives. For instance, one might suggest regional boards similar to the ration and draft boards of the war period, or the possibility of state control might be introduced as an alternative to federal regulation. Perhaps citizens' committees would hold most appeal for the population. One might also include further issues. For example, do listeners favor a periodic review of program content? And by whom should this be carried out: A government agency, the industry, a board of experts? Or do they feel that the scheduling of specific program types should be controlled in any way? We recall from earlier sections of this report that parents disapprove of the possible effects of crime and mystery programs on their children. There have been some suggestions that these programs should be broadcast only late in the evening after children have gone to bed, and indeed one of the networks has made this its policy. How many listeners agree that this should be a general policy for all stations and who should see that it is carried out? Finally, it might be profitable to find out how respondents feel about the coverage of local news and matters of local interest. Should this be subject to regulation of some kind, and, again, by whom? It might turn out that the role of regional boards and local citizens' committees would be most prominent in connection with this last issue.

These few suggestions make it obvious that any thorough

study of demands for social control would require a full-fledged survey. At the moment we must content ourselves with a further analysis of the material already at hand. Table 37 selects those people who favor some kind of regulation of any of the five issues and indicates their preference for either government control or self-regulation by the industry. The order of the issues is somewhat different from that in Table 36. We have arranged them here so that the issues on which government control is *least* favored are at the top of the list; those on which government control is *most* favored are at the bottom of the list.

TABLE 37

PROPORTIONS OF RESPONDENTS RECOMMENDING GOVERNMENT CONTROL AS OPPOSED TO SELF-REGULATION BY THE INDUSTRY*

	Gov't.	Radio Industry	Total
Not too much advertising is broadcast on the radio.............	19%	81%	= 100%
Each station broadcasts a certain number of educational programs	27	73	= 100
Radio stations regularly carry programs giving both sides of public issues......................	29	71	= 100
Radio news broadcasts are accurate......................	37	63	= 100
The profits of radio stations aren't too high....................	49	51	= 100

* Among those respondents who favored some kind of regulation.

The most conspicuous result of this table is that the two economic issues are found at opposite ends of the list. In the first step of our analysis, when we asked listeners whether they favored *any* kind of regulation, answers on these two issues were virtually identical: 78 per cent called for some controls on the amount of radio advertising; 76 per cent called for some regulation of station profits. The situation is very different when we ask who should be entrusted with these powers and duties of regulation. On the profits issue one-half of the respondents, more than on any other question, call for government controls; on the advertising issue less than one-fifth, the smallest number, do so. This finding is probably not as strange as it may seem at first glance. First of all, it is not surprising that many individuals who want to see station profits limited recommend that the controls be imposed from outside. The industry itself could not be expected to forego profits unless it was required to do so by an external agency. Secondly, government regulation may be suggested only as a last resort, when it would be unrealistic to count on self-regulation or some other kind of nongovernmental control.[2] Because listeners are not particularly hostile toward radio advertising, most of them are willing to let the industry regulate the number of commercial announcements which are broadcast. Perhaps also reflected in this result is the feeling that since radio is supported by advertising revenue, it is up to the industry to decide how

---

[2] Although we have no direct evidence that government controls are recommended as a last resort, we have some data which make it seem plausible. As with the eight statements about commercials, it was possible here to construct a kind of index. Each individual was given five opportunities to suggest that government controls should be imposed on the radio industry. Once his answers were recorded, we could determine how frequently he took these opportunities, and thus assign a score, ranging in value from 0, meaning government recommended on no issue, to 5, meaning government suggested on all five issues. When we examined the distribution of these score values in our total sample, we found that approximately 50% had a score of 0—approximately one-half of the respondents suggested government controls on none of the five issues. But the listeners were given a similar number of opportunities to suggest self-regulation by the industry, which made it possible to obtain a comparable score value for each individual's preference for industry regulation. Here the distribution was quite different. Only 20% of the sample failed to suggest industry control on at least one of the issues.

much advertising is needed to maintain current programming standards.[3]

Respondents take less extreme positions on the three issues which we previously labeled "moral." On the one hand, they feel less frequently than in the case of advertising that these are matters for self-regulation; on the other hand, they recommend government controls less frequently than they did on the issue of profits. Again we find some variation within this relatively homogeneous group of statements. Two of them—the supply of educational programs and the guarantee of air time for both sides on any issue—are matters of program scheduling. These, the respondents seem to feel, are more properly left to self-regulation. Where news accuracy is involved, however, they are somewhat more anxious to see the government take a hand. This may in some way be an expression of distrust, of fear that radio stations will bias news in favor of their advertisers or their own interests. It may be that respondents feel that they can trust the industry to schedule its programs fairly and intelligently, but that they cannot be so confident when matters of news content are involved. These are mere speculations, however; our data permit us to state such interpretations in only the most tentative form.

Personal Concern and Social Control

There are two aspects of Table 37 which deserve further attention. One concerns the role of government control in general. Some readers may feel that the relatively small vote cast for government regulation is due to the way in which the question was worded. Actually the present wording is the

---

[3] There is some evidence in our survey that respondents see a link between advertising and high standards of radio. Approximately 10% said that they prefer commercial radio to a license-fee system, because "sponsored programs are better," "the government wouldn't pay top price for big artists," and so on. See also Paul Lazarsfeld and Harry Field, *The People Look at Radio*, p. 23. Chapel Hill: The University of North Carolina Press, 1946.

end-result of considerable experimentation.[4] During the course of our pretesting, when different alternative wordings were tried, we found a remarkably constant reaction to all questions on government supervision. The results of our survey are closely paralleled in other studies.[5] From all of this we can assume that attitudes toward government regulation are very stable ones, not easily swayed by minor variations in the wording of questions.

The American public lends strong support to the *status quo*. If they were asked whether mail delivery or tax collection should be turned over to private companies, most of them would say no. Conversely, if services customarily in private hands were under discussion, the very large majority would reject the suggestion that they be taken over by the government. The reader who regrets this fact will easily find explanations which reconcile his social convictions with the survey findings. It would be sheer self-deception to believe that the result itself is an artifact of question wording. It is quite safe to say that, at the present time, no question which suggests increased governmental activity in business affairs would get anything but a small sprinkling of pro-government answers.[6]

---

[4] See Appendix D.

[5] For such comparisons see "The Quarter's Polls" in the *Public Opinion Quarterly*, where the wording of, and answers to, various questions on government regulation, among other topics, is regularly reported.

[6] There is some evidence, in fact, that the notion of public ownership or control has become somewhat less popular during the last two years. In both the earlier and present surveys we asked our respondents, "Which do you think would be better for the people in this country—if the (banks, food stores, coal mines, radio stations, newspapers, gas and electric companies) were run by the government or by private business?" At both times a majority of the samples voted for private business in all of these industries, but the majority was even larger in the present survey. The comparative figures are shown in Table 27, Appendix C. We might interpret this change in the following way: During the war, people were impressed by the way in which the government handled all problems of war production and distribution. Now, several years after hostilities ended, this memory

In this connection there is one observation which is of interest. We have seen previously that the poorly educated and low income groups are generally less critical of radio than are high income groups. But, probably because of their political and social philosophies, respondents lower on the social scale are somewhat more in favor of government regulation. They have less to lose by any changes in the social system, and are therefore more receptive to the notion of controls and regulation by the government. This can best be seen by classifying respondents according to the conventional A-B-C-D ratings and then studying the "regulation scores" which we explained in a footnote on page 93. Although the A-B-C-D ratings are not an exact statement of income, we know from much research experience that the D people are of a lower socio-economic status than the C people and the C people are in turn lower than the A and B individuals. (The A and B groups are combined here in order to obtain a sufficiently large number of cases for our analysis.) Table 38 shows that as we go down the socio-economic ladder, we find

TABLE 38

ATTITUDES TOWARD GOVERNMENT REGULATION OF RADIO ACCORDING TO SOCIO-ECONOMIC STATUS

Number of issues on which government controls recommended:	SOCIO-ECONOMIC STATUS		
	A and B	C	D
None of issues................	55%	51%	47%
One or two issues.............	30	31	31
Three or more issues	15	18	22
	100%	100%	100%

has worn off, and the traditional American belief that private business is more efficient has come to the fore once again.

consistently more people who favor more government regulation in the radio field.

Although there are these differences in attitude, the lower income groups indicate that, by and large, they too support the *status quo*. Nearly half of the D people favor no government controls at all; only slightly more than one-fifth favor government regulation on three or more of the five issues.

A reader who finds the results of this survey in agreement with his own attitudes should not go too far in believing that the population supports his convictions in every detail. One well-known fact about social attitudes is that general statements of policy often receive a very different measure of support than do proposals for specific action.[7] This is particularly true when the issue is one to which little detailed thought has been given, as is undoubtedly the case with attitudes toward government ownership or regulation. The question which we asked was a general one, but there are a number of specific points on which the respondents could be interviewed. We could, for example, determine their reactions to possible advantages of public ownership— greater job security, less danger of depression, lower prices, and so on. When these advantages were identified as possible by-products of public ownership, people would support government control very much more frequently than they do on a general question. For what they now reject probably is the slogan "government regulation," a phrase which has many negative connotations for the American people.

This is an interesting psychological problem. It may lead to confusion, however, for some readers may feel that we are now contradicting what we said in previous paragraphs about the stability of attitudes toward government regulation despite variations in question wording. Actually they are two separate points. The first is that general over-all

[7] See *Gauging Public Opinion*, p. 22 (edited by Hadley Cantril). Princeton: Princeton University Press, 1944.

attitudes will remain the same, no matter what wording is used. If we ask whether the government should "run" or "control" or "regulate" or "own" we shall find very constant answers. The second point, the one which we have just considered, is that when the implications or consequences of government ownership are spelled out, when we talk of specific rather than general issues, the results will be very different.

We can mention these problems only in passing. Our primary purpose in doing so is to make sure that neither side in this vital controversy will take our figures as a final indication of "what the people want." Further and more systematic investigation is needed. The questions do lend themselves, however, to the kind of revealing comparisons which we have reported in preceding pages.

They can serve still another purpose. Through them we can show that the more interested or the more concerned a respondent is with any particular phase of radio, the more likely he is to request some sort of social control on that specific issue. What evidence have we for this point?

On three of the five issues we not only have information on the extent to which respondents favor regulation, but we also have independent data on the degree of their concern with the matter. Let us first consider radio advertising. All of the various questions which we discussed in Chapter IV provide us with indices of concern, for we can assume that there is a direct relationship between critical attitudes toward commercials and concern with the amount of advertising broadcast. The more severely critical a respondent is, the more likely it is that he will find the present amount of advertising excessive. This in turn will lead him to favor some kind of regulation. Using the "criticism score" for this analysis we find that our expectations are borne out. As Table 39 indicates, the higher the criticism score, the more frequent are requests for controls on the amount of advertising.[8]

---

[8] This holds true even when amount of education is held constant.

TABLE 39

PROPORTION WHO FAVOR REGULATION OF
ADVERTISING ACCORDING TO
CRITICISM SCORE

	CRITICISM SCORE		
	I (+)	*II*	*III* (−)
Proportion who say that "somebody" should regulate amount of advertising..........................	64%	78%	91%

Virtually all of the critics, then, want some limits on the amount of air time devoted to commercial announcements.[9]

We should expect further that the critical listeners will less frequently entrust the regulation of radio advertising to the industry itself. They will feel that only an outside agency, the government in this case, can be counted on to comply fully with their request for controls. Here again the data bear out our expectations. In Table 40 the listeners who favor some regulation of advertising have been separated according to their criticism scores, and their preferences for either government controls or self-regulation are examined. We find that as criticism increases so does the frequency with which the government is asked to impose controls.[10]

There are other areas of radio where this same relationship between personal concern and demand for social control

----

[9] Table 39 is also interesting for another reason: It provides further insights into the attitudes of those whom we classified as the partisans of radio commercials. Nearly two-thirds of them, the people who had low criticism scores, want someone to see to it that "not too much advertising is broadcast on the radio." In the light of this finding perhaps the best way of characterizing them would be to say that they are tolerant of commercials at the present time, but of course they would not like to hear unlimited amounts of radio advertising.

[10] This relationship persists when education is held constant.

TABLE 40

PREFERENCES FOR GOVERNMENT CONTROL OF
ADVERTISING AS OPPOSED TO
SELF-REGULATION ACCORDING
TO CRITICISM SCORE*

	CRITICISM SCORE		
Regulation should be left to:	*I* (+)	*II*	*III* (−)
Government..................	13%	18%	24%
Radio Industry..............	87	82	76
	100%	100%	100%

* Among those people who favored some kind of regulation.

exists. One of the issues, we recall, dealt with regulation of
the supply of educational programs. But which of the
listeners are concerned with this matter? Fortunately, there
was a question in our survey which permits us to separate
them out. They are the people who say that they "wish
there were more serious programs." As with the critics of
radio advertising, their interest in this particular phase of
radio's operations predisposes them to favor regulation more
frequently than the less highly motivated listeners. Because of
the close relationship between education and demand for
serious programs, we must control level of schooling in our
analysis. The main result of our analysis will be found by
reading across the rows of Table 41. This shows that, on all
educational levels, the listeners who want more serious programs are also more anxious to see this supply regulated by
some agency.

Once more the table reveals additional insights into
social attitudes. When we look down the columns, we find
further corroboration for our earlier statement (see Table
38 on page 96) that individuals low on the social scale are

TABLE 41

PROPORTION WHO FAVOR REGULATION OF EDU-
CATIONAL BROADCASTS ACCORDING TO
PURPOSE IN LISTENING AND
EDUCATION

Per cent who feel that somebody
should regulate number of
educational programs

PURPOSE IN LISTENING

Education:	Mostly for Entertainment	Both Entertainment and Serious	Want More Serious
College.............	79%	84%	92%
High School........	87	91	95
Grade School.......	90	92	94

more inclined to favor regulation of radio. The one exception to this general statement is that those who are vitally
concerned with the issue, in this case those who say they want
more serious programs, favor regulation even when the
notion runs counter to their general philosophies. No matter
what their educational level, the vast majority of serious
listeners want some controls. In other words, we can say that
when an issue is important enough to them, individuals will
recommend policies which they would reject in general
application.

Interestingly enough, however, serious listeners call on
the government to impose controls only slightly more frequently than do other groups of listeners. The differences
are so slight, in fact, that they had best be disregarded. The
respondents may feel that once they have made their desires
known, the industry itself should be free to decide precisely

how many educational programs are to be offered and when they are to be broadcast.

There is a final aspect of radio for which we have information regarding both degree of personal concern and willingness to see some kinds of controls imposed: This is the issue of fairness. We recall that one of the statements on regulation asked the respondents whether they thought that "someone should see to it that radio stations regularly carry programs giving both sides of public issues." Also, in another part of the interview we asked the respondents whether they felt that radio actually was fair. Here we have two questions which permit us to study the relationship between personal interest and attitudes toward regulations.

On this issue, however, the relationship is somewhat different than in the other two cases. For reasons which are understandable, those who express relatively little concern, those who find radio fair, favor regulation no less than do the respondents who are concerned: 93 per cent of the listeners who consider radio fair, as compared with 96 per cent of those who do not, feel that "somebody" should impose controls. When we concentrate only on this first step in our analysis, we can see that the question is a kind of catch-all; it is hard to imagine anyone saying that there should be no guarantee of impartiality in programs on public issues.

The really crucial question, however, is whether the two groups recommend the same kinds of controls. That is, do the concerned listeners recommend self-regulation less frequently than the unconcerned? Here once more we can anticipate the findings. It is radio advertisers and station owners, we remember, who are held responsible for radio's unfairness; other groups are blamed in only a negligible number of cases.[11] This being so, we should expect that outside agencies will be called on to impose the controls, for if it is "insiders" who are now responsible for unfairness,

---

[11] See Chapter III, p. 56.

self-regulation cannot be counted on. Table 42 confirms these speculations: Government controls are suggested much more frequently by those who find radio unfair.

TABLE 42

PREFERENCE FOR GOVERNMENT CONTROL OF FAIRNESS AS OPPOSED TO SELF-REGULATION ACCORDING TO JUDGMENT OF FAIRNESS*

	Radio is:	
Regulation should be left to:	Fair	Unfair
Government	23%	38%
Radio Industry	77	62
	100%	100%

* Among those who favor some kind of regulation.

The listener who is critical of any feature of radio is more likely to favor regulation, and usually he is more likely to favor regulation by the government. There is evidence, however, that when the industry does respond to listeners' requests, criticisms decrease in number. In our earlier survey one-third of the listeners felt that radio stations were not broadcasting enough news about local events and issues. Partly because of this finding, the industry made efforts to increase its coverage of local news. As a result, we now find, two years later, that less than one-quarter of the respondents complain that there is not enough local news.[12]

These findings have practical implications as well as psychological interest. It seems unlikely at the present time that there will be a strong popular movement for further control of radio; but the situation might change and such a

[12] For the complete results on this question, see Table 28 in Appendix C.

movement become more probable if listeners are not satisfied on those issues with which they are particularly concerned. If they felt that their requirements were not being met, there might be a considerable increase in the number who wanted stricter controls and controls imposed from outside the industry.

So far we have discussed two major points. We have identified the critics of radio and have suggested the role which they should play in the progressive development of radio standards. Secondly, we have seen what is expected of the industry itself. Listeners favor regulation on a number of issues, but, for the most part, they leave it to the industry to decide what steps should be taken in connection with each of these matters. We found that this general statement had to be qualified in one major respect, however: When listeners are particularly concerned with a specific issue, they are less likely to count on self-regulation and more likely to recommend outside controls.

Considerations of what the critic can do and what the industry itself can do still leave the picture incomplete. No program of development can be successful without the active encouragement and support of the great mass of listeners themselves. In the last analysis, whatever is done depends on them.

The Listener's Task

Broadcasters will be very gratified by the way in which their audience expresses satisfaction on virtually every point about which they were asked. But is this all that can be expected of the listener? Doesn't the broadcaster make a legitimate request when he asks that his listeners also show an interest in radio developments, that they keep themselves informed about what is going on in the radio field?

Progressive leaders in the industry know that radio is a young medium, much too young to have its scope and functions rigidly defined. They also know that the longer radio continues along its present routes, both good and bad, the more likely it is that it may become set in its ways. Changes and innovations may be increasingly resisted; radio may be defined by what is current practice rather than by what is possible. Far-sighted broadcasters therefore look to the audience for help in preserving radio's flexibility and receptiveness to change. They want listeners to show an open-mindedness toward innovations; to approve of the industry's experimentation, even though they may not like some of the experimental programs; to demonstrate a flexibility in their listening habits. This kind of flexibility, of course, requires awareness of new developments on the air-waves.

We attempted to find out just how well the audience was fulfilling these responsibilities. The picture is not an encouraging one. It requires special efforts to keep abreast of new developments on the radio scene, and unfortunately few listeners make the necessary efforts. This is shown in Table 43. Only a minority of the audience makes an effort

TABLE 43

"Do you usually make a special effort to find out about new programs on the radio?"

Yes	35%
No	65
	100%

to keep informed, and therefore only this minority is in a position to encourage the industry in its efforts to introduce new ideas. The other two-thirds leave it pretty much to chance whether or not they learn of new programs.

Just because there are so few listeners who exhibit this laudable curiosity about new programs, it seems worth while to wonder who can be counted on to encourage and support innovations introduced by the industry. Offhand we should expect two factors to play an important part in getting people to shop around on the air-waves: One is interest, indicated by amount of radio listening, and the other is general alertness, indicated by formal education.[13] Table 44, which analyzes the role of these two factors, shows that interest is far more important.

TABLE 44

PROPORTION WHO MAKE AN EFFORT TO FIND NEW PROGRAMS ACCORDING TO EDUCATION AND AMOUNT OF EVENING LISTENING*

| | Per cent who make an effort | | |
Amount of evening listening:	College	High School	Grade School
Less than 1 hour	24%	22%	19%
1–3 hours	36	33	35
3 or more hours	51	49	45

* We use amount of evening listening, since most men are unavailable at other times of the day.

It is somewhat surprising that listeners with college training make only slightly greater efforts to keep themselves informed of what is going on in radio. There are other situations in which the educational differences would undoubtedly be much greater—efforts to find out what books are being published or what plays are being produced on Broadway, for example. Radio listening seems to be one type of behavior which does not call into play the greater alertness and curiosity usually associated with more formal education.

The fact that less interested listeners make fewer efforts to follow new developments has serious implications for the

---

[13] There is another possible factor: Knowledge of the availability of other programs. A listener who lives in an area served by only one station, to take an extreme example, will probably make few efforts to find out about developments on the air. Since he has little choice in what he hears, attempts to learn of new programs will not be of any particular benefit.

radio industry. The people who listen only occasionally to the radio are more likely to be critical.[14] They listen less partly because current radio programs do not appeal to them especially, but also because they have various misconceptions as a result of their infrequent exposure. These misconceptions might be corrected if the light listeners were kept informed of what was going on in radio, particularly if they were kept informed of innovations and additions to the program schedule. But, as we have seen, it is just these people, those who are least interested in radio at the present time, who make the least effort to find out about new developments. There is further evidence for this in the fact that listeners who feel that radio is doing a "fair" or "poor" job in the community make fewer efforts than do those who feel that radio's performance is "excellent." Forty-four per cent of the latter group, 34 per cent of those who feel that radio is doing a "good" job, and only 32 per cent of those who think it is "fair" or "poor" make any special efforts to find out about new programs. From the standpoint of the radio industry, this represents a vicious circle.

Not only general interest but also specific listening habits and tastes should make some persons more eager than others to look for new programs. American radio caters mainly to the listeners who want to be entertained. Consequently those who make up the market for serious programs must search systematically for the programs they enjoy. Have the serious listeners acquired the appropriate habits? Do they make special efforts to find the kinds of programs they say they want? Only to a small extent. Table 45 compares the efforts made by the serious listeners with those made by the people who listen mainly for entertainment and those who listen for both reasons. The individuals who want more serious programs are somewhat more anxious than the "entertainment-minded" listeners to find new programs, but the difference is small.

---

[14] See Chapter III.

TABLE 45

PROPORTION OF RESPONDENTS MAKING AN
EFFORT TO FIND NEW PROGRAMS
ACCORDING TO THEIR PURPOSE
IN LISTENING

Purpose in listening:	Per cent who make an effort
Mostly for entertainment..........	30%
Both, now satisfied................	37
Want more serious programs.......,	39

There are some groups of listeners who are relatively
active in searching out new programs: These are the well
educated and serious-minded listeners, the fans, and those who
feel that radio's performance is good. But not all, or even
most, of these respondents try to keep themselves informed
about radio developments. Consequently the over-all picture
shows a majority of listeners failing in what might be considered their responsibilities to the radio medium.

Why is this the case? Why do so few individuals try to
find out about new programs? One possible explanation is
that such efforts are not part of our tradition—that it is not in
the "folkways" of our society to be curious about non-
technical developments in the radio field. Ours is a mechan-
ically minded and gadget-conscious society. We feel it
important to know about the latest technical developments
in television or FM, just as we feel it important to know about
the new features in a late model automobile. But we do not
experience the same curiosity or concern with "cultural"
developments. This fact may be deplored, but the evidence
for it in our own lives is so convincing that it cannot be
easily overlooked.

There is a second explanation: Even when the listener

is appropriately motivated to look for news about radio, he seems to have difficulties in obtaining it. For, paradoxically enough, radio, the medium which might logically be expected to supply this information, is not particularly well equipped to do so, and the other media do not fill the breach at the present time.

In a curious way radio is what we might call "time-bound." This fact is so obvious that we need only remind the reader of what we mean. First of all, radio waits for no one. If an individual is not beside his radio when a program or announcement is broadcast, or if he misunderstands or forgets it, it is lost to him forever (unless, of course, it is rebroadcast at another time.) Radio listening has none of the flexibility which is possible in newspaper reading or movie going. The broadcaster sets the pace, and the listener either does or does not follow him. Secondly, radio, more than the other mass media, is limited—by time—in the amount of material which it can produce. The printed media can use various space-saving devices to increase the content of their issues; a minute or two more or less makes little difference in a film. The broadcast day proceeds with split-second timing. A minute

---

TABLE 46

SOURCES OF INFORMATION ABOUT NEW PROGRAMS*

Newspapers	45%
Just by dialing around	33
Radio announcements	26
Friends or relatives	24
Magazines	3
Other	1
Don't find out	10

* Figures do not add to 100% because each respondent was permitted more than one answer.

spent in promoting an addition to the radio schedule means a minute less for some other kind of announcement.

In view of these difficulties, it is not surprising that listeners depend heavily on non-radio sources for their information about radio. All of our respondents, those who make special efforts as well as those who do not, were asked, "How do you usually learn about new programs?" Table 46 indicates the sources which they reported.

When we consider both aimless dialing from one station to another and listening to announcements, we see that radio is still the most important single source of information about programs, but newspapers run a close second. The recommendations of friends and relatives are the only other ways in which listeners learn of new programs.

The difficulties which radio encounters in guiding its listeners clarify other findings in our survey. The greater the efforts which listeners make to find out what is going on in radio, the more will they rely on newspapers for their information, and the less will they depend on the casual discoveries they might make in dialing from one station to another. In other words, the people who are most anxious to

TABLE 47

SOURCES OF INFORMATION ACCORDING TO EFFORT TO FIND NEW PROGRAMS*

Sources	Make Effort	Don't Make Effort
Newspapers.................	73%	30%
Dialing around..............	24	37
Radio announcements........	38	19
Friends or relatives..........	20	25
Magazines.................	6	2

* Figures do not add to 100% because each respondent was permitted more than one answer.

keep themselves informed about radio turn more frequently
to non-radio sources. These findings are reported in Table 47.
The results are remarkably consistent. Observe, for example,
that the two groups differ markedly in the way in which
they use radio as a source of information. Among the actively
interested people casual dialing along the radio band is less
frequent than is listening to station announcements. Among
the less interested listeners the relative importance of these
two sources of information is just reversed: They rely more
on a sampling of programs on the air, and less on announcements of programs to be broadcast at a later time.

Other findings point to the same conclusions. All of the
respondents who said that their daily newspapers carried
program logs were asked how frequently they consulted
them. Over half of the listeners who make an effort to keep
informed refer to the listings every day; about one-third of
those who make no efforts consult newspaper listings "seldom
or never."[15] Our respondents were also asked whether their
newspapers printed columns of radio news and gossip, and,
if so, how often they read them. Here again the more active
listeners indicated their greater dependence on newspapers.
Over a third of those who make efforts to learn about new
programs read these newspaper columns every day, whereas
this is true for less than one-fifth of the inactive listeners.[16]

Although newspapers are undoubtedly in a better position than radio to provide information on new programs, and
although our data indicate that there is a real demand and
need for such information, we can question whether the job
is being done adequately. Even a casual inspection of the daily
press will show that readers can find relatively little about
radio. To be sure, virtually all readers can find listings of
radio programs, in their daily newspapers—when asked about
it, 92 per cent of our respondents said that their favorite
papers carried such listings. But these are hardly a help.

---

[15] See Table 29 in Appendix C.
[16] See Table 30 in Appendix C.

Almost invariably they are nothing more than station logs, in small print and on a back page. Intelligible classified guides to listening are seldom provided. Furthermore, columns of radio news and criticism are rare; or if they are not rare, they are at least obscure. When we asked our respondents whether their newspapers carried such columns, only one-half answered affirmatively; nearly one-third were uncertain whether radio columns were available in their favorite papers, and the remaining 22 per cent were sure they were not.

If newspapers think of radio stations as their main competitors for advertising revenue, it will not be easy for them to allocate more space to news of radio. But publishers have always felt it their duty to provide information about developments in any field, whether it is movies, crime, or foreign news. Our survey indicates that the American public does consider radio an important field and that, furthermore, it looks to the press to give news about this field. In the long run newspapers will find it to their advantage to provide better information about radio, for it will improve their circulation and will make their news coverage more complete. Several large newspapers have already started along this path, and it is to be hoped that others will follow suit.

In the meantime, broadcasters will have to do as much as possible to build their audiences themselves. Perhaps many people in the industry do not realize how limited the knowledge of individual listeners actually is. Studies have revealed that it sometimes takes months before the audience finds out about a new program. A person who listens to the radio a great deal is not necessarily "radio conscious." The research student can only indicate a point of weakness; it is up to the creative person in the industry to devise ways of developing radio consciousness among his listeners. Perhaps he should not restrict himself to spot anouncements of new programs, for these may become lost in the multitude of commercial messages. Perhaps dramatized "previews" of new programs or listener quizzes on radio matters might prove more effective. Whatever the methods used, the present survey indicates that audience building should have priority on the agenda of all broadcasters.

This brings us to the end of our discussion. We have studied general communications behavior, and particularly, radio program preferences. We have seen how well people appraise the general job that radio is doing. Even its most controversial feature—advertising—is accepted by the majority of American people. Yet there is criticism coming from a minority which deserves to be heard. These critics usually look to the industry to bring about the improvements which they request. We have seen, finally, that the masses of listeners do little to keep themselves informed about new developments on the radio scene, perhaps because of their general satisfactions.

In such an atmosphere of contentment it is fortunate indeed that broadcasters themselves want to be kept on their toes. Radio is still the only industry which periodically surveys people's attitudes and then frankly publishes the findings. It can only be hoped that this triple alliance of research, vigilant criticism, and creative leadership will continue; that it will bear fruit in terms of desirable improvements; and that it will be taken as an example by other communications industries.

QUESTIONNAIRE AND RESULTS

Questions 1 to 3 were asked of all persons interviewed.

$$100\% = 3,529$$

Ques. *1.* *A.* "Do you have a radio in working order?
   B. Do you usually read a daily newspaper?
   C. Do you usually read a weekly newspaper?
   D. Do you read any magazines regularly?"

	Working Radio	*Daily Newspaper*	*Weekly Newspaper*	*Magazines*
Yes..........	91%	90%	40%	61%
No............	9	10	60	39

$$100\% = 3,529$$

Ques. *2.* "In every community, the schools, the newspapers, the local government, each has a different job to do. Around here, would you say that the schools are doing an excellent, good, fair, or poor job? How about the newspapers? The radio stations? The local government? The churches?"

	Schools	*Newspapers*	*Radio Stations*	*Local Government*	*Churches*
Excellent....	13%	9%	14%	4%	22%
Good........	46	54	56	38	54
Fair.........	21	24	18	31	13
Poor........	4	5	4	11	2
Don't know..	16	8	8	16	9

$$100\% = 3,529$$

Ques. 3. "Which do you think would be better for the people in this country—if the (*each industry below*) were run by the government, or by private business?"

	Banks	Food-stores	Coal Mines	Radio Sta-tions	News-papers	Gas and Elec-tric Com-panies
Govern-ment....	28%	14%	32%	9%	6%	24%
Private business..	55	76	49	77	85	65
Don't know	17	10	19	14	9	11

100% = 3,529

Questions 4 to 17 were asked of radio owners only.

100% = 3,225

Ques. 4. "Where do you get most of your daily news about what is going on—from the newspapers or the radio?"

Newspapers.......... 48%
Radio................ 44
Don't know.......... 8

100% = 3,225

Ques. 5. "Do you ever feel like criticizing . . .
   A. When you read your newspaper?
   B. When you see a movie?
   C. When you listen to the radio?"

Sometimes feel like criticizing:

	Newspaper	Movies	Radio
Yes.......	68%	57%	67%
No........	32	43	33

100% = 3,225

(If "YES" on radio) "What are some of your main criticisms of the radio? Any others?"

	Proportion of Owners[1]	Proportion of Critics[1]
Advertising, commercials......	26%	43%
Mystery, crime plays.........	15	24
News and commentators......	10	16
Daytime serials..............	9	14
Music, poor quality, not enough, and so on..................	5	8
Miscellaneous and other.......	14	23
General criticisms, referring to all radio..................	7	11
Nothing in particular, don't know.....................	4	6
100% =	3,225	2,161

Ques. 6. "I'd like to ask you how *fair* radio stations and newspapers generally are. For example, do you think radio stations are generally fair in giving both sides of public questions? How about newspapers in general?"

	Radio Stations	Newspapers
Fair.........	79%	55%
Not fair.....	13	37
Don't know..	8	8
100% =	3,225	

[1] When reporting questions asked of only a part of our total sample of radio owners, we shall give two sets of percentages. One of these uses the total number of radio owners (3,225 people) as the base; the other uses only the subgroup questioned as the base (in this case the 2,161 respondents—called "critics"—who said they sometimes feel like criticizing radio).

(If radio stations not fair) "Who do you think is chiefly responsible for this—the radio station owner, the commentator or announcer who gives the news, the advertisers who sponsor the news programs, or someone else?"

	Proportion of Owners	Proportion of Critics
Station owners................	3%	26%
Commentator or announcer...	2	18
Advertisers..................	4	32
Someone else................	2	12
Don't know.................	2	12
100% =	3,225	419

(If newspapers not fair) "Who do you think is chiefly responsible for this—the newspaper owner, the columnist or reporter, the advertisers in the paper, or someone else?"

	Proportion of Owners	Proportion of Critics
Newspaper owner............	19%	53%
Columnist or reporter........	6	16
Advertisers..................	3	7
Someone else................	5	13
Don't know.................	4	11
100% =	3,225	1,193

Ques. 7. *A.* "As far as your own listening is concerned, is the radio giving too much time, about the right amount, or not enough time to . . .

(1) News about other countries?
(2) News about this country?
(3) News about things around here?"

	1. Other Countries	2. This Country	3. Local Events
Too much..........	16%	3%	2%
About right........	59	65	67
Not enough........	16	26	24
Don't know.........	9	6	7

100% = 3,225

B. "How about the newspapers you read? Do they give too much space, about the right amount, or not enough to . . .

(1) News about other countries?
(2) News about this country?
(3) News about things around here?"

	1. Other Countries	2. This Country	3. Local Events
Too much..........	14%	2%	2%
About right........	64	72	73
Not enough........	12	19	18
Don't know........	10	7	7

100% = 3,225

Ques. 8. "Which one of these four statements comes closest to what you yourself think about advertising on the radio?"

A. I'm in favor of advertising on the radio.. 32%
B. I don't particularly mind advertising on the radio............................ 35
C. I don't like advertising on the radio, but I'll put up with it.................... 22
D. If it were up to me, I'd cut out all advertising on the radio.................... 9
   Don't know........................ 2

100% = 3,225

Ques. 9. "Here are some comments that have been made about radio advertising or commercials. I'd like to know which ones you agree with and which ones you disagree with."

	Agree	Dis- agree	Don't Know	100% = 3,225
A. Commercials spoil the program by interrupting it	60%	36%	4%	100%
B. Commercials give useful information about things you want to buy	74	22	4	100
C. Commercials are boring and repetitious	58	35	7	100
D. Commercials are noisy and distracting	46	49	5	100
E. Commercials are worth while because they tell who pays for the program	65	26	9	100
F. Commercials claim too much for the product	60	28	12	100
G. Commercials are often amusing and entertaining	63	32	5	100
H. Commercials are often in bad taste	46	42	12	100

Ques. 10. "How do you feel about *singing* commercials? In general, do you like them better than the straight commercials, or not as well?"

Better............... 37%
Not as well........... 43
No difference......... 18
Don't know.......... 2

100% = 3,225

Ques. 11. "As you know, there are other countries like England where everybody who owns a radio set pays a license fee and there is no advertising on the radio. Suppose you could get your present radio programs without any advertising in them if you paid a license fee of $5 a year. Would you rather have the advertising or would you rather pay the $5 fee?"

A. (If "YES") Would it be worth a fee of $10 a year?

B. (If "YES" to *A*) Would it be worth a fee of $25 a year?

Would pay:

$25 a year....................	2%
$10 a year but not $25.........	7
$5 a year but not $10..........	11
Total who would pay fee.......	20%
Would prefer advertising.......	76
Don't know..................	4

100% = 3,225

Ques. 12. "Do you think that somebody—either the Federal government or the radio industry itself—should see to it that (*each item below*) . . ."

FOR EACH ITEM ANSWERED "YES": "Who do you think should do that—the Federal government, or the radio industry itself?"

	No-body	Federal Govern-ment	Radio Indus-try	Don't Know	100% = 3,225
(1) Not too much advertising is broadcast on the radio?....	22%	13%	54%	11%	100%
(2) The profits of radio stations aren't too high?...........	24	27	28	21	100
(3) Radio stations regularly carry programs giving both sides of public issues?......	7	23	58	12	100
(4) Each station broadcasts a certain number of educational programs?.........	10	21	57	12	100
(5) Radio news broadcasts are accurate?...............	7	30	52	11	100

Ques. 13. "On an average weekday, about how many hours do you listen to your radio . . ."

    A. In the morning—from 6 a.m. to noon?

    B. In the afternoon—from noon to 6 p.m.?

    C. In the evening—after 6 p.m.?

	Morning	Afternoon	Evening	Total
None, don't listen...	29%	38%	5%	2%
Up to 15 minutes....	6	3	1	1
16–30 minutes......	11	8	4	2
31–60 minutes......	20	17	16	6
Over 1 hour to 2 hours..........	15	17	27	14
Over 2 hours to 3 hours..........	10	8	22	16
Over 3 hours to 4 hours..........	5	4	16	13
Over 4 hours to 5 hours..........	3	2	7	10
Over 5 hours to 6 hours..........	1	3	2	10
Over 6 hours.......	*	*	*	26

$$100\% = 3,225$$

* Less than 1 per cent.

Ques. 14. A. "Here's a set of cards listing different kinds of radio programs. Would you mind looking through those cards, and telling me the types of programs you like to listen to in the daytime?"[a]

    B. "Now which types of programs there do you like to listen to in the evening?"[a]

	Daytime	*Evening*
News broadcasts...........	72%	74%
Comedy programs..........	*	59
Quiz and audience participation	27	56
Dance and popular music....	33	49
Complete dramas (other than mystery).................	*	46
Mystery programs...........	*	41
Talks or discussions about public issues..................	22	44
Semiclassical music..........	22	33
Sports programs............	23	33
Serial stories...............	39	*
Classical music.............	16	30
Homemaking programs......	30	*
Religious programs..........	34	21
Hillbilly and western music...	23	26
Talks on farming...........	16	*
Livestock and grain reports...	14	*

100% = 3,225

a More than one answer was permitted.
* Heard infrequently at the designated time.

Ques. 15. "Do you usually make a special effort to find out about new programs on the radio?"

Yes................ 35%
No.................. 64
Don't know.......... 1

100% = 3,225

Ques. 16. "How do you usually learn about *new* radio programs?"*

Newspapers.......... 45%
Just by dialing........ 33
Radio announcements.. 26
Friends and relatives... 24
Magazines........... 3
Other................ 1
Don't find out........ 10

100% = 3,225

* More than one answer was permitted.

Ques. 17. "Of course, most people listen to news broadcasts on the radio. But which one of these statements best describes the way you yourself use the radio for other types of programs?"

A. I listen to the radio mostly for entertainment and very seldom listen to serious or educational programs.................... 26%

B. I like to listen to both serious and entertainment programs, and I'm satisfied with what I get now.................... 52

C. I like to listen to both serious and entertainment programs, but I wish there were more serious programs.................20

Don't know................ 2

100% = 3,225

Factual items were asked of all persons interviewed.

100% = 3,529

Item 1. NEWSPAPER READERSHIP

"Do you usually read a daily newspaper?"   (See Question 1-*B* above)

A. (If "YES") "Is there a listing of radio programs in the paper?"

Yes.................. 92%
No.................. 4
Don't know.......... 4

100% = 3,176

(1) (If "YES" to *A*) "How often do you refer to the program listings in the newspapers?"

	Proportion of Readers	Proportion Who Have Listings
Every day...........	31%	34%
2–3 times a week.....	20	22
Less than that........	16	17
Seldom or never......	25	27
100% =	3,176	2,921

B. (If "YES" on item 1) "Is there a special column in the paper which gives news and gossip about radio?"

Yes..................	49%
No	22
Don't know	29
100% = 3,176	

(1) (If "YES" to *B*) "How often do you read this column?"

	Proportion of Readers	Proportion Who Have Columns
Every day...........	12%	24%
2–3 times a week.....	10	20
Less than that........	10	21
Seldom or never......	17	35
100% =	3,176	1,556

Item 2. Movie Attendance

"About how many times did you go to the movies during the last month?"

Not at all............ 39%
Once................. 15
Two or three times.... 22
Four or five times..... 15
More than five times... 9

100% = 3,529

Item 3. Book Reading

"Did you happen to read any books during the last month?"

Yes.................. 26%
No.................. 74

100% = 3,529

A. (If "YES") "About how many books did you finish reading during the last month?"

Read no books........ 74%
Read one book........ 9
Read two books....... 7
Read three books...... 4
Read four books....... 2
Read five or more..... 4

100% = 3,529

B. (If "YES") "Where did you get the last book you read?"

	Proportion of Total Sample	Proportion of Book Readers
Bought it...................	8%	32%
Borrowed from friend........	6	23
Public library...............	5	19
Home collection of books.....	2	8
Rental library...............	2	8
Gift........................	1	4
Other......................	1	4
Don't remember............	1	2
	100% = 3,529	918

Item 4. THE HUCKSTERS

A. "Have you read *The Hucksters?*"
B. "Did you happen to see the movie?"

Only read the book.... 8%
Only saw the movie.... 14
Both read the book and
saw the movie....... 5
Exposure to neither.... 73

100% = 3,529

Item 5. "By and large, do you take things pretty much as they come, or are you more likely to be bothered when things don't go right?"

Take as they come..... 61%
More likely bothered... 37
Don't know.......... 2

100% = 3,529

Other factual information is reported in Appendix B, which deals with the characteristics of the sample.

APPENDIX B

CHARACTERISTICS OF THE SAMPLE

The National Opinion Research Center of the University of Chicago, which made this survey at the request of the National Association of Broadcasters, is an academic institution, formerly at the University of Denver. It used its own national staff of personally trained interviewers who are scattered throughout the United States. The 3,529 personal interviews represent a cross section of the United States adult population. Well-established laws of probable error indicate that this number of interviews are accurate within about 2 per cent of true opinion.

The characteristics of respondents with and without radios are shown in the tables which follow.

APPENDIX TABLE I

SCOPE OF SAMPLE

Total Persons Interviewed...............		3,529
Total with radios in working order........	3,225	
Total without working radios............	304	

APPENDIX TABLE 2

CHARACTERISTICS OF THE SAMPLE

	TOTAL SAMPLE		RADIO HOMES	
	Number	*Per Cent*	*Number*	*Per Cent*
Total persons interviewed..	3,529	100%	3,225	100%
Sex				
Male.................	1,736	49%	1,568	49%
Female...............	1,792	51	1,656	51
Not ascertained.........	1		1	
Age				
21–29.................	740	21%	696	22%
30–39.................	875	25	812	25
40–49.................	777	22	723	23
50–59.................	573	16	522	16
60 and over...........	557	16	465	14
Not ascertained.........	7		7	
Economic level				
A (Wealthy)...........	62	2%	60	2%
B (Prosperous).........	460	13	450	14
C (Middleclass).........	1,894	54	1,800	56
D (Poor)..............	1,107	31	911	28
Not ascertained.........	6		4	
Education level				
Completed college.......	259	7%	250	8%
Some college..........	368	10	355	11
Completed high school...	878	25	846	26
Some high school........	740	21	690	22
Completed grade school..	655	19	587	18
Some grade school.......	565	16	458	14
No schooling...........	53	2	29	1
Not ascertained.........	11		10	

APPENDIX TABLE 2—*Continued*

CHARACTERISTICS OF THE SAMPLE

Size of community	TOTAL SAMPLE		RADIO HOMES	
	Number	Per Cent	Number	Per Cent
Metropolitan district over				
1,000,000.............	1,019	29%	957	30%
Metropolitan district under				
1,000,000............	860	25	815	25
2,500–50,000............	539	15	495	15
Under 2,500............	535	15	479	15
Farm.................	576	16	479	15
Geographic region				
Northeast.............	998	28%	944	29%
Middlewest...........	1,115	31	1,026	32
South.................	968	28	834	29
West.................	448	13	421	13

The 1945 and the 1947 samples are very similar in their characteristics.[1] In economic level, educational level, and geographic region they are virtually identical. However, the 1947 sample contains somewhat more men, and slightly more younger people. (Size of community is not directly comparable, since different systems of classification were used in the two studies.)

---

[1] For a comparison of the two samples, compare the figures here with those in Appendix A of Paul Lazarsfeld and Harry Field, *The People Look At Radio*. Chapel Hill: The University of North Carolina, 1946.

Appendix C

SUPPLEMENTARY TABLES

The following tables are those referred to at different points in the text.

Appendix Table 3

PROPORTION OF MOVIE FANS* ACCORDING TO AGE, SEX, AND MARITAL STATUS

Age:	MALE		FEMALE	
	Single	*Married*	*Single*	*Married*
21–29............	58%	38%	44%	32%
30–39............	42	23	31	24

---

* *Movie fans* are those who saw four or more movies in previous month.

Appendix Table 4

PROPORTION CHECKING DANCE MUSIC AS A FAVORITE RADIO PROGRAM ACCORDING TO MOVIE ATTENDANCE AND AGE

Age:	MOVIES SEEN DURING PREVIOUS MONTH		
	None	*1–3 Movies*	*4+ Movies*
21–29....................	45%	50%	53%
30–49....................	29	32	39
50 and over..............	15	18	21

131

APPENDIX TABLE 5

AMOUNT OF RADIO LISTENING ACCORDING TO SEX

Amount of evening listening:	Male	Female
Less than 1 hour	30%	20%
1–3 hours	50	49
3 or more hours	20	31
	100%	100%

APPENDIX TABLE 6

AMOUNT OF RADIO LISTENING ACCORDING TO AGE

	AGE		
Amount of evening listening:	21–29	30–49	50 and Over
Less than 1 hour	20%	24%	27%
1–3 hours	48	49	45
3 or more hours	32	27	28
	100%	100%	100%

APPENDIX TABLE 7

AMOUNT OF RADIO LISTENING ACCORDING TO SIZE OF COMMUNITY

	SIZE OF COMMUNITY				
Amount of evening listening:	Metropolitan Districts Over One Million	Metropolitan Districts Under One Million	2,500 to 50,000	(Under 2,500) Rural Non-Farm	Farm
Less than 1 hour.	24%	22%	26%	29%	27%
1–3 hours........	48	48	52	47	55
3 or more hours..	28	30	22	24	18
	100%	100%	100%	100%	100%

APPENDIX TABLE 8

PROPORTION OF RESPONDENTS WHO SAW NO MOVIES IN PREVIOUS MONTH ACCORDING TO SEX, AGE, AND SIZE OF COMMUNITY

	Per cent who saw no movies					
	MEN			WOMEN		
	21–29	30–49	50 and Over	21–29	30–49	50 and Over
Large metropolitan districts........	11%	27%	52%	22%	26%	45%
Cities and towns....	14	31	60	18	30	59
Rural.............	23	46	75	30	41	68

APPENDIX TABLE 9

PROPORTION WHO READ BOOKS ACCORDING TO AGE AND EDUCATION

	AGE		
	21–29	30–49	50 and Over
Education:			
College....................	57%	52%	45%
High school..............	31	27	28
Grade school....	1	10	10

APPENDIX TABLE 10

PROPORTION WHO READ MAGAZINES ACCORDING TO AGE AND EDUCATION

	AGE		
	21–29	30–49	50 and Over
Education:			
College....................	81%	89%	80%
High school..............	64	69	65
Grade school.............	44	44	34

APPENDIX TABLE 11

PROPORTION OF HEAVY LISTENERS* ACCORDING TO AGE AND EDUCATION

	AGE		
	21–29	30–49	50 and Over
Education:			
College....................	18%	20%	17%
High school..............	36	28	28
Grade school.............	33	29	31

* *Heavy listeners* are those who listen to the radio three or more hours on an average weekday evening.

APPENDIX TABLE 12

PROPORTION OF HEAVY LISTENERS* ACCORDING TO SEX, AGE, AND SIZE OF COMMUNITY

	MEN			WOMEN		
Size of Community:	21–29	30–49	50 and Over	21–29	30–49	50 and Over
Large metropolitan districts........	24%	19%	21%	46%	36%	25%
Cities and towns....	38	20	18	40	34	24
Rural.............	22	20	11	30	28	18

* *Heavy Listeners* are those who listen to the radio three hours or more on an average weekday evening.

APPENDIX TABLE 13

CORRELATION BETWEEN EDUCATION AND INTERVIEWERS' RATINGS OF SOCIO-ECONOMIC STATUS

Interviewers' Ratings:	College	High School	Grade School
A and B............	38%	13%	5%
C.................	53	63	43
D.................	9	24	52
	100%	100%	100%

APPENDIX TABLE 14

EVENING PROGRAM PREFERENCES ACCORDING TO AGE AND EDUCATION *

	COLLEGE			HIGH SCHOOL			GRADE SCHOOL		
	21–29	30–49	50 and Over	21–29	30–49	50 and Over	21–29	30–49	50 and Over
News broadcasts	75%	78%	83%	72%	75%	79%	61%	70%	74%
Comedy programs	70	59	49	72	64	57	55	52	51
Quiz and audience participation	51	56	57	60	61	62	46	53	47
Popular and dance music	66	56	29	68	56	32	56	46	29
Complete dramas	61	55	46	51	39	43	44	42	32
Discussions of public issues	59	63	67	33	45	54	21	37	36
Mystery programs	56	41	21	53	45	32	59	42	27
Semiclassical music	55	48	50	28	36	36	14	20	25
Sports programs	47	37	35	41	35	34	25	32	3
Classical music	53	50	61	21	27	36	15	21	24
Hillbilly and western music	10	8	19	24	22	20	42	39	38
Religious programs	11	14	28	9	17	29	11	25	36

* Percentages do not add to 100% in any of these columns because more than one answer was permitted each respondent.

Appendix Table 15

EVENING PROGRAM PREFERENCES ACCORDING TO SEX AND AMOUNT OF EVENING LISTENING*

	Less than 1 hour		1–3 hours		3 or more hours	
	Men	Women	Men	Women	Men	Women
Program types preferred by women:						
Quiz and audience participation.........	37%	40%	56%	62%	65%	71%
Complete dramas.................	25	28	43	53	58	64
Semiclassical music..............	23	27	31	37	35	42
Program types preferred by men:						
News broadcasts.................	70%	55%	81%	74%	87%	78%
Comedy programs................	43	32	68	62	73	72
Discussions of public issues.........	46	23	52	42	57	44
Sports programs.................	40	10	52	16	59	30
Hillbilly and western music...........	22	19	31	24	32	25

* There were no consistent sex differences on program types not listed here.

APPENDIX TABLE 16

EVENING PROGRAM PREFERENCES ACCORDING TO
VETERAN STATUS AND AGE*

(Males Only)

	21–29 years old		30–39 years old	
	Veterans	Nonveterans	Veterans	Nonveterans
News broadcasts	71%	68%	77%	72%
Comedy programs	26	27	28	28
Quiz and audience participation	53	58	58	58
Popular and dance music	65	66	58	55
Complete dramas	49	54	40	53
Discussions of public issues	40	35	50	44
Mystery programs	53	55	48	45
Semiclassical music	36	29	33	35
Sports programs	58	28	54	22
Classical music	26	27	28	28
Hillbilly and western music	24	23	19	25
Religious programs	11	9	14	17

* As in previous tables on program preferences, these figures do not add to 100% because each respondent was permitted more than one answer.

APPENDIX TABLE 17

EVENING PROGRAM PREFERENCES ACCORDING TO SIZE OF COMMUNITY*

	Large Metropolitan Districts	Cities and Towns	Rural
News broadcasts................	76%	73%	73%
Comedy programs..............	60	60	57
Quiz and audience participation..	49	59	53
Popular dance music...........	51	51	44
Complete dramas..............	50	47	40
Discussions of public issues......	51	42	41
Mystery programs..............	46	41	38
Semiclassical music............	39	33	25
Sports programs...............	38	34	27
Classical music................	40	28	23
Hillbilly and western music......	19	25	33
Religious programs.............	16	23	24

* Figures do not add to 100% because more than one answer was permitted.

APPENDIX TABLE 18

PROPORTION WHO PREFER SERIOUS PROGRAMS AND PROPORTION WHO PREFER ENTERTAINMENT ACCORDING TO AGE AND EDUCATION

	College	High School	Grammar School
21–29 years	25% / 31%	30% / 14%	42% / 12%
30–49 years	17% / 33%	29% / 16%	31% / 16%
50 years and over	16% / 29%	21% / 18%	25% / 18%

KEY:

☐ = Per cent who prefer entertainment programs

☐ = Per cent who want more serious programs

APPENDIX TABLE 19

RELATIONSHIP BETWEEN CRITICISM OF DIFFERENT MEDIA

A) CRITICISM OF RADIO AND NEWSPAPERS:

	Occasionally Critical of Newspapers	Never Critical of Newspapers
Occasionally critical of radio...	82%	34%
Never critical of radio........	18	66
	100%	100%

B) CRITICISM OF RADIO AND MOVIES:

	Occasionally Critical of Movies	Never Critical of Movies
Occasionally critical of radio..	73%	26%
Never critical of radio........	27	74
	100%	100%

C) CRITICISM OF NEWSPAPERS AND MOVIES:

	Occasionally Critical of Movies	Never Critical of Movies
Occasionally critical of news-papers....................	72%	24%
Never critical of newspapers...	28	76
	100%	100%

APPENDIX TABLE 20

PROPORTION WHO FEEL THAT RADIO IS "UNFAIR" ACCORDING TO OVER-ALL APPRAISAL OF RADIO AND OCCASIONAL CRITICISM

Per cent who say radio is "unfair"

	Excellent, Good	Fair, Poor
Occasionally critical of radio....	13%	23%
Never critical of radio.........	7	13

APPENDIX TABLE 21

JUDGMENT OF RADIO'S FAIRNESS ACCORDING TO AMOUNT OF EVENING LISTENING

	AMOUNT OF EVENING LISTENING		
	Less Than 1 Hour	1–3 Hours	3 Hours or More
Radio is fair................	73%	80%	84%
Radio is unfair..............	15	12	12
Don't know................	12	8	4
	100%	100%	100%

APPENDIX TABLE 22

JUDGMENT OF RADIO'S FAIRNESS ACCORDING TO SOCIO-ECONOMIC STATUS

	A and B	C	D
Radio is fair....................	81%	79%	78%
Radio is unfair.................	14	14	11
Don't know....................	5	7	11
	100%	100%	100%

APPENDIX TABLE 23

JUDGMENT OF RADIO'S FAIRNESS ACCORDING TO OCCUPATION

	Professionals, Owners and Managers	White Collar Workers	Laborers	Farmers and Farm Labor
Radio is fair.......	79%	76%	79%	82%
Radio is unfair.....	17	19	14	13
Don't know.......	4	5	7	5
	100%	100%	100%	100%

APPENDIX TABLE 24

AGREEMENT AND DISAGREEMENT WITH ARGUMENTS ABOUT RADIO COMMERCIALS

	Agree	Dis-agree	Don't Know	Total
Negative Statements				
Commercials spoil the program by interrupting it....	60%	36%	4%	100%
Commercials claim too much for the product..........	60	28	12	100
Commercials are boring and repetitious...............	58	35	7	100
Commercials are noisy and distracting..............	46	49	5	100
Commercials are often in bad taste....................	46	42	12	100
Positive Statements				
Commercials give useful information about things you may want to buy.........	74%	22%	4%	100%
Commercials are worth while because they tell who pays for the program..........	65	26	9	100
Commercials are often amusing and entertaining......	63	32	5	100

APPENDIX TABLE 25

PROPORTION WHO READ *THE HUCKSTERS* AC-
CORDING TO EDUCATION AND NUMBER
OF BOOKS READ DURING PREVIOUS
MONTH

During previous month read:	Per cent who read *The Hucksters*		
	College	High School	Grade School
No books	17%	9%	2%
One book	25	18	4
2–3 books	41	29	6
4–or more books	49	33	21

APPENDIX TABLE 26

PROPORTION WHO SAW MOVIE, *THE HUCKSTERS*,
ACCORDING TO EDUCATION AND MOVIE
ATTENDANCE IN PREVIOUS MONTH

During previous month saw:	Per cent who saw *The Hucksters*		
	College	High School	Grade School
No movies	11%	5%	1%
1–3 movies	25	27	13
4 or more movies	47	40	29

APPENDIX TABLE 27

"Which do you think would be better for the people in this country—if the (*each industry below*) were run by the government, or by private business?"

	Coal Mines		Banks		Gas and Electric Companies		Radio Stations		Newspapers	
	1945	*1947*	*1945*	*1947*	*1945*	*1947*	*1945*	*1947*	*1945*	*1947*
Government.....	40%	32%	33%	28%	30%	24%	16%	9%	10%	6%
Private business.	47	49	54	55	58	65	70	77	83	85
Don't know......	13	18	13	17	12	11	14	14	7	9
	100%	100%	100%	100%	100%	100%	100%	100%	100%	100%

APPENDIX TABLE 28

"As far as your own listening is concerned, is the radio giving too much time, about the right amount, or not enough time to news about things around here?"

	1945	1947
Too much............................	2%	2%
About right..........................	57	67
Not enough..........................	33	24
Don't know..........................	8	7
	100%	100%

APPENDIX TABLE 29

FREQUENCY OF REFERRING TO RADIO LISTINGS IN NEWSPAPERS ACCORDING TO EFFORTS TO FIND OUT ABOUT NEW PROGRAMS*

	Make Special Efforts	Make No Efforts
Refer to listings:		
Every day..................	52%	25%
2–3 times a week.............	27	21
Less than that...............	12	20
Seldom or never.............	9	34
	100%	100%

* Among those who say their newspapers carry such listings.

APPENDIX TABLE 30

FREQUENCY OF READING RADIO COLUMNS IN NEWSPAPERS ACCORDING TO EFFORTS TO FIND OUT ABOUT NEW PROGRAMS*

Read columns:	Make Special Efforts	Make No Efforts
Every day	36%	17%
2–3 times a week	25	17
Less than that	19	22
Seldom or never	20	44
	100%	100%

* Among those who say their newspapers print such columns.

DEVELOPMENT OF THE QUESTIONNAIRE

The questionnaire used in the present study was developed by a group of radio researchers working in cooperation with social psychologists, sociologists, and others interested in social research. Since a primary purpose of the present study was to provide data which could be compared with that obtained three years ago, the interview schedule used in the 1945 study served as the starting point. Even though many questions were taken over intact from the earlier investigation, the present schedule went through nine editions before it was accepted as final and sent into the field. In many of these, suggested questions and revised wordings were pretested with small samples selected and interviewed by the National Opinion Research Center. The results of these pretests were then used as the basis for further revisions and modifications.

This appendix is designed to explain how the final series of questions was decided on, why some questions were tried and eliminated, and why some were not included even in the pretesting. Perhaps it would be best to start with a review of the interview schedule used in the first study (1945) and explain why some of the questions were not repeated this time. It should be noted at the outset that there was never any intention of making the present study an exact duplicate of the earlier one. The research committee agreed that some of the questions should be retained so that trends in attitudes toward radio could be determined. In addition, there were

---

[1] This appendix was first drafted by Kenneth H. Baker, research director of the National Association of Broadcasters, and secretary of the research committee which developed the present questionnaire.

some topics, felt to be important, which had not been covered in the 1945 study. In order to include questions on these without making the interview overly long and involved it became necessary to delete some questions from the first schedule.

Below, then, are the questions from the first study, together with an indication of the considerations which determined whether or not they were to be retained.

QUESTIONS ASKED IN 1945

Ques. 1.

    A. "Do you have a radio in working order?"
    B. "Do you usually read a daily newspaper?"
    C. "Do you usually read a weekly newspaper?"
    D. "Do you read any magazine regularly?"

All four parts of this question were retained, both because they permitted us to study trends and because they provided data essential to the analysis of other questions.

Ques. 2.

"Taking everything into consideration, which one of these do you think did the best job of serving the public during the War—magazines, newspapers, moving pictures, or radio broadcasting?"

This question was omitted from the present study at the start. It is topical in nature, and answers that it yielded would have been of questionable value.

Ques. 3.

"In every community the schools, the local government, the newspapers, each has a different job to do. Around here would you say that the schools are doing an excellent, good, fair, or poor job? How about the newspapers? The radio stations? The local government? The churches?"

In order to study trends of interest to broadcasters, this question was retained in exactly the same form. It appears as Question 2 on the 1947 schedule.

Ques. 4.

    A. "From which one source do you get most of your daily news about what is going on—the newspapers or the radio?"

    B. "Which one gives you the latest news most quickly?"

    C. "Which one gives you the most complete news?"

    D. "Which one gives you the fairest, most unbiased news?"

Part A of this question was retained and appears as Question 4 in the 1947 schedule. Parts B and C were eliminated, because there was no reason to expect any change from the findings of the 1945 study or from the results of other studies on the subject. Part D, however, was elaborated and appears in the 1947 schedule as Question 6. This change seemed advisable, because the 1945 question did not provide an opportunity for the respondents to say whom they held responsible for unfairness. It was felt that answers to such a question would have bearings on the current issue of editorializing over the radio.

Ques. 5.

    "In what ways do you think radio news could be improved?"

It was decided not to repeat this question, because the results it yielded in the 1945 study were of little value. Other questions (especially Questions 6 and 7) in the 1947 schedule investigate opinions about radio news more directly.

Ques. 6.

    "As far as your own listening is concerned, is the radio giving too much time, about the right amount, or not enough time to news about other countries?—news about this country?—news about things around here?"

In view of the useful information obtained from answers to this question in 1945, it was repeated in the new schedule. In addition the same questions were asked about news in the newspapers, in order to provide a basis of comparison. In the 1947 schedule, these two questions appear as Parts A and B of Question 7.

Ques. 7.
"If you had to give up either going to the movies or listening to the radio, which one would you give up?"

Ques. 8.
"If you had to give up either reading the newspapers or listening to the radio, which would you give up?"

These questions were not repeated since there was no reason to believe that the answers would differ materially from those obtained in many other surveys using the same or similar questions. In addition, the 1947 schedule included other questions permitting more valuable comparisons between radio and newspapers. The "miss most" type of question was tried in a pretest and discarded because it showed nothing new.

Ques. 9.
"On the average weekday, about how many hours do you listen to the radio during the daytime—that is, before six o'clock in the evening?"

Ques. 10.
"And on the average weekday, about how many hours do you listen to the radio after six o'clock in the evening?"

These two questions were combined into one (Question 13) on the 1947 schedule. In addition, the day was divided into three segments—morning, afternoon, and evening—instead of the two used in 1945. It was fully realized that this method of asking the question inflates the total amount of listening slightly, but the three-part division of the day gives broadcasters more useful information about their daytime audience. Furthermore, we recognized that the new wording of the question would prevent us from studying trends in total amount of listening between 1945 and 1947.

Ques. 11.
A. "Here's a set of cards listing different kinds of radio programs. Would you mind looking through these cards and telling me the types of programs you like to listen to in the daytime?"
B. "Now which types of programs there do you like to listen to in the evening?"

For a number of reasons this question was repeated as Question 14 in the 1947 schedule: (1) It permitted us to study changes in taste, (2) station managers and program directors are interested in the results, and sales managers find them useful, and (3) it is a type of question which the respondent seems to enjoy answering. Certain minor alterations in the classifications of programs were made in the 1947 schedule. These include a slightly different subdivision of musical programs, the elimination of children's programs from the list (since only adults were interviewed), and so on.

Ques. 12.
"Are there any kinds of programs that aren't on the air when you'd like to listen to them? If so, what kinds of programs, and at about what time would you like to hear them?"

This question was not repeated in the 1947 schedule because it elicited few specific suggestions in 1945. Other questions in the 1947 schedule (especially Questions 15, 16, and 17) were intended to unearth specific dissatisfactions with programming and also to bring to light the same type of information obtained by the older question.

Ques. 13.
"Are there any kinds of programs you would like to hear more of? If so, what kinds are they and at about what time would you like to hear them?"

Ques. 14.
"Are there any kinds of programs you would like to hear fewer of? If so, what kinds?"

In the 1945 study the answers to both of these questions revealed little of value or practical usefulness to the broadcaster. With the exception of daytime serials, mentioned by 16 per cent of the respondents in answer to Question 14, no significant number of listeners stated that they would like to hear more or less of the various categories of radio programs. Both questions were therefore eliminated from the present schedule.

Ques. 15.

"Aside from news, in what other fields does the radio add to your information and knowledge?"

Because of limitations on the length of the interview, this question had to be dropped from the 1947 schedule. It was felt that little would be gained by repeating it.

Ques. 16.

"As far as you know, is the radio broadcasting in England run any differently from the way it is here? If so, what is the main difference?"

A pretest of this question in 1947 showed as much misinformation on this matter as had been found in 1945. (About two-thirds answered "Don't know.") As a result, it was decided not to use the question again in its old form, since it permitted little analysis. Another question (Question 11) in the 1947 schedule *tells* the respondent what one of the major differences between American and British radio is, and then asks his opinion. (See p. 121.)

Ques. 17.

"Do you ever feel like criticizing when you listen to the radio? If so, what are some of your main criticisms?"

This question, admittedly a leading one, was retained in the 1947 schedule both to permit trend comparisons and to search out the foci of criticism. It was elaborated, however, to include also some indication of similar critical attitudes toward newspapers and movies. The free-answer part of the question, "If so, what are some of your main criticisms?" was asked only in connection with radio listening, however, in order to keep the question from becoming too involved and cumbersome. (Furthermore, pretests of the question revealed that criticisms of newspapers revolved mainly around the matter of bias which was covered in Question 6 of the 1947 questionnaire.) The elaborated question appears in the 1947 schedule as Parts A, B, and C of Question 5.

Ques. 18.

"As far as you know, where do radio stations get the money to run them?"

Ques. 19.

"As you know, every radio station broadcasts many different programs each day. About how many of these programs would you say are sold to advertisers—all of them, about three-quarters of them, about half of them, about one-fourth, or less than that?"

These questions were not repeated in the 1947 schedule since there was no basis for believing that the answers would vary significantly from those obtained in the 1945 study.

Ques. 20.

A. "If your newspaper could be produced without advertising, would you prefer it that way?"

B. "If your radio programs could be produced without advertising, would you prefer it that way?"

Some readers of the first study criticized these questions on the grounds that they presented an unrealistic picture to the respondent and then asked for an impossible choice. Furthermore, it was felt that it took more time and space than desirable to probe the "reasons why" underlying answers to the questions. Accordingly, they were not included in the present questionnaire. Other questions in the 1947 schedule, notably Questions 8, 9, and 11, are directed toward the same attitudes, but in a more direct and realistic way.

Ques. 21.

"Which one of these four statements comes closest to what you yourself think about advertising on the radio?"

A. I'm in favor of advertising on the radio, because it tells me about the things I want to buy.

B. I don't particularly mind advertising on the radio. It doesn't interfere too much with my enjoyment of the programs.

C. I don't like the advertising on radio, but I'll put up with it.

D. I think all advertising should be taken off the radio.

Critics of the first study had objected to the wording of these alternative statements. Accordingly, several recordings were pretested in the 1947 schedule, and the question retained with those changes in wording which were acceptable to both critics and respondents. This item now appears as Question 8 in the 1947 schedule.

Ques. 22.

"Would it be worth it to you to pay a tax of $5 a year to get radio programs without any advertising in them? If so, would it be worth a tax of $10 a year? If so, would it be worth a tax of $25 a year?"

This question was combined with Questions 16 and 20 of the 1945 schedule, and appears now as Question 11 of the 1947 schedule. The wording has been changed slightly to make the alternative more meaningful, and to include information about British broadcasting not known to so many respondents.

Ques. 23.

"Can you give me an example of what you think is the best advertising you have heard on the radio?"

Ques. 24.

"Can you give me an example of what you think is the worst advertising you have heard on the radio?"

Ques. 25.

"Here are some criticisms of radio advertising, or commercials. Would you tell me which ones, if any, you feel strongly about?"

It is always difficult to analyze and summarize statistically the answers to such questions. Accordingly, they were not repeated in the 1947 study. Instead, the results which had been obtained in 1945 were used as the basis for developing a new set of questions, incorporating the major arguments pro and con advertising on the radio. These appear in the 1947 schedule as the different parts of Question 9.

Ques. 26.
"Are there any products listed here (on card) which you think should not be advertised over the radio?"

Ques. 27.
"Do you think that radio stations should sell time for the following things (a list of organizations and activities), or should they give the time free, or shouldn't they be on the air at all?"

Since there was no reason to believe that answers to these questions would have changed in the past two years, and since there was no further interest in repeating the questions, they were not included in the 1947 schedule.

Ques. 28.
"As far as you know, does the government have anything to do with the operation of radio stations? If so, which powers *does* the Federal government have, and which powers *should* it have?"

This question has been reworded and is included as Question 12 of the 1947 schedule. In the first place, it was too long in its original form; the list of powers asked about was therefore reduced. Secondly, the original question did not permit the respondent to reply that somebody other than the Federal government could or should exercise the powers listed; acordingly, other alternatives, namely the radio industry and "nobody," were included.

Ques. 29.
"As far as you know, does the government require radio stations to broadcast a certain number of religious and educational programs or do the stations broadcast these voluntarily?"

Since there was some ambiguity in the interpretation of answers to this question, it was repeated in the 1947 schedule in a slightly altered form, Part 4 of Question 12.

Ques. 30.
"I'd like to ask you how fair you think radio stations, newspapers, and magazines generally are. For example, do you think radio stations are generally fair in giving both sides

of an argument? How about newspapers in general? Magazines?"

The issue in this question is included in Question 6 of the 1947 schedule.

To summarize, then, the research subcommittee began its efforts to develop the 1947 schedule with a careful examination of the 1945 questionnaire. Some of the earlier questions were retained, for one or both of the following reasons:

(1) Repetition of the question would provide valuable information concerning trends in attitudes toward radio. (See especially Questions 3, 4A, 6, and 30 in the 1945 schedule.)

(2) The questions provided information basic to the analysis and interpretation of other data. (See especially Questions 1, 9, 10, and 11 in the 1945 schedule.)

Questions contained in the 1945 schedule were eliminated from the 1947 questionnaire for any one or more of these reasons:

(1) There was no reason to believe that the distribution of answers would have changed between 1945 and 1947, and there was no further interest in repeating the question. (See especially Questions 4B and 4C, 18, 19, 26, and 27 in the 1945 schedule.)

(2) The question had not worked satisfactorily in the 1945 study, so that it was either changed or elaborated before inclusion in the 1947 schedule. (See especially Questions 12, 13, 14, 20, 28, and 29 in the 1945 schedule.)

(3) The question was topical in nature, so that it no longer applied or was meaningful in the later time period. (See especially Question 2 in the 1945 schedule.)

In addition to this careful screening of the 1945 questionnaire, the research subcommittee sought to determine what other issues or questions might be included in the 1947 schedule. To this end they solicited suggestions from various individuals who were both professionally and casually interested in the matter of public opinion toward radio. The result of these inquiries was that a number of questions were submitted for consideration, each of which received the careful attention of the subcommittee.

One of the chief factors determining whether a question was to be included was its length, or, rather, the amount of interview time that would be required to answer it. It was generally acknowledged that an interview of the type contemplated should not consume more than 30 or 40 minutes. If a given question threatened to require a disproportionate amount of time, it was discarded—not because it was not a suitable matter for investigation, but because the interview schedule did not permit its inclusion.

Another factor determining whether a question would be included was the amount of sophistication or erudition requested from the respondent. If it could be anticipated or discovered through pretesting that respondents were not generally familiar with the matter under investigation, there seemed to be little point in questioning them about it. Instead, it was felt that a full study devoted to that one issue alone might well be undertaken at another time. An example of a question on which the public shows an amazing lack of information was the following:

"As far as you know, which of the following powers does the government have over the radio stations?
1. To decide how much advertising can be broadcast.
2. Give each station a regular place on the dial.
3. Decide who should be allowed to own a station.
4. Decide what kinds of programs should be broadcast.
5. Limit the profits of radio stations.
6. See that the radio stations regularly carry programs giving both sides of public issues.
7. Make sure that each station broadcasts a certain number of educational programs.
8. See to it that news broadcasts are accurate."

The use of this question in 1945 revealed that half or more than half of the respondents were either uninformed or misinformed on each of these matters. Pretests of the same question in the preparation of the 1947 schedule indicated that the people are still as uninformed on these matters as they were in 1945. There seemed to be little point, then, in repeating the question again at this time.

Still another consideration was the clarity of the question. If it seemed that respondents were not clear as to what type of information was being sought in any particular question—regardless of the level of their own information—it was not included.

An example of a series of questions which were excluded from the 1947 schedule for several of these reasons were those concerned with editorializing by the licensee. This matter is currently of great interest to the broadcasting industry and in recent months it has received considerable attention from all quarters. The subcommittee was anxious to include it in the 1947 schedule if at all possible. Several attempts to develop one or two questions which would determine the public's stand on this matter were all unsuccessful, however. Illustrative of the attempts were these questions:

> "As you know, each newspaper has an editorial page or policy which presents the views of that paper on important local, national, and international issues.
>
> (*a*) Do you think that the newspapers *should* express their own point of view on such matters?
> (*b*) Do the radio stations in your locality express their own point of view?
> (*c*) Do you think the radio stations in your locality *should* express their own point of view on such matters?"

and

> "Which do you think it is better for owners of radio stations to do—just broadcast the opinions of other people on public questions, or should they also present their own point of view?"

Interviewers' reports on the use of these questions indicated:
(1) difficulty in getting respondents to understand what was
being talked about, and (2) a belief on the part of the public
that the editorial point of view of a commentator or analyst
carried by a station reflected the point of view of the station
licensee. Although about three-fourths of the respondents felt
that radio stations should have the right to express their own
points of view, the question was not included in the final draft
of the 1947 schedule. Instead, it was felt that the subject
might well be a matter for separate investigation through an
interview devoted wholly or nearly so to this one issue alone.
It was apparent that much of the interview time in such a
study would necessarily have to be spent in clarifying the
issue and presenting the facts.

Another type of question which met difficulty in the pretesting was that which asked the respondent to compare
present-day radio offerings with something he might very
well have forgotten. Such questions require feats of psychological manipulation which many respondents simply
cannot handle. The following question, for instance, was
asked in an early pretest:

> "During the past few years, would you say that radio
> advertising has been improving, or getting worse, or is it
> about the same? How about newspaper advertising? How
> about magazine advertising?"

The results of this question in the pretest indicated that about
three-fourths of the people think that advertising is either
"about the same" or "improving" in all three mass media,
except, possibly, radio. When the comments were examined,
however, they suggested that the respondents had difficulty
in remembering advertising of several years ago and that
therefore they had difficulty in making valid comparisons
with the advertising of today. The issue obviously needs a
more elaborate introduction and a wording which is psychologically more sound.

Another type of question which was included in the

pretesting but dropped because it involved too much time or was, rather, worthy of separate study, was the one directed at determining what kind of job radio is doing in certain specified areas of entertainment or information. This question was asked:

> "How good a job do you think radio is doing in providing programs for housewives—excellent, good, fair, or poor? How about programs of serious music? How about entertainment for the whole family? How about programs of discussion on public issues?"

It was felt advisable to eliminate this question from the final draft of the 1947 schedule, because interviewers reported having a great deal of difficulty with it. It did not provide for the type or length of answer which the respondent wanted to give and became most unwieldy as part of a long interview on a variety of subjects.

Still another type of question which was not included in the final draft was that in which there was so little division of opinion that the answers offered little challenge or additional help from the standpoint of their contributions to cross-tabulations. Examples of this type of question are the following:

> "Do you think that radio stations should have the right to broadcast meetings and hearings of Congress that are open to the public?"

Over 90 per cent of the respondents answered this question affirmatively. Another question of this type was:

> "Some people say advertising is good for the country because it creates demand for things and raises our standard of living. Other people say advertising is bad because it makes things cost more and is often exaggerated. In general, how do you feel about it—is advertising a good thing or a bad thing for this country?"

Over 80 per cent of the respondents thought advertising a good thing; over 10 per cent had no opinion. These questions could be of little value in cross-tabulations because of their failure to divide the respondents into useful subgroups. Furthermore, they add little which could not be deduced from the answers to others which were both shorter and more pertinent.

Some of the "reason why" subquestions were eliminated from the final draft of the schedule. This was done either because they added nothing, respondents being unable to tell *why* they answered as they had, or because they had already accomplished in the pretests their purpose of making sure that the question was properly understood. It is a well-known fact that many people are unable to verbalize the details of an opinion or belief, that many of the reasons for certain attitudes are not known to those who hold them. The other role of the "reason why" questions—to help the interviewer determine whether the respondent understands the question— was well served in several instances and was, as a matter of fact, the basis for eliminating some of the questions discussed above.

Attempts to determine what the public thinks about radio's development of new talent or new types of programs were also unsuccessful. One of the questions was:

"As far as your own listening is concerned, is radio developing enough new *kinds* of programs?"

Answers to this question were difficult to evaluate. Respondents would, for instance, say "Yes" and then, when asked for an example of what they meant, cite a well-known program type that had been on the air for years. What they meant, apparently, was that—as far as they were concerned— radio was doing a good job of developing more programs of a type which they happened to like especially. It was decided that this issue, although an important one in much of present-day radio criticism, would have to be eliminated from the 1947 schedule in the hope that it could be taken up more adequately in a separate study.

In summary, then, new questions suggested for inclusion

in the 1947 schedule were eliminated for any of a variety of reasons:

(1) The question was too long for inclusion in an interview in which it was hoped not one but several issues could be dealt with.

(2) The question was not understood by the respondent or else he was not familiar with the issue to which the question was directed. Both conditions would require more time than could be afforded in the "education" of the respondent.

(3) Answers in the pretest showed such a preponderance in one direction or another that they would serve no useful purpose from the standpoint of dividing listeners into meaningful subgroups.

Appendix E

LATENT ATTRIBUTE ANALYSIS

At two points in this study we made use of new developments in the general field of "attitude scaling." Analyses of this kind made great advances during the war through the work done by the Research Branch of the Morale Services Division of the Army.[1] This is not the place to discuss details of such techniques. A general picture can be given by tracing briefly the steps leading to the graph which indicated the relative severity of different arguments about radio commercials. (See Graph II, p. 70.)

The first problem in such an analysis is to determine whether the five comments belong to the same psychological dimension, whether there is really something like an "attitude toward commercials." This is done by studying how the five items are related to each other. Any two items form a fourfold table, similar to the one we presented on the relationship between listening to daytime serials and to mystery programs (see p. 31 of the text). The five comments about commercials yield ten such relationships and, for each of them, we can determine how likely it is that people who endorse one criticism will also endorse the second. In this kind of problem, the so-called "cross-product" is used as an index.

We therefore present a table of these ten relationships which may tell us whether there is any regularity in the relations between the five comments. The comments, and the proportion of the sample agreeing with them, were:

---

[1] A general report by the former director of the Research Branch, Samuel S. Stouffer, and his associates will soon be published by the Princeton University Press.

1. Commercials are boring and repetitious 58.2%
2. Commercials are noisy and distracting 45.8
3. Commercials spoil the program by interrupt- ing it 59.6
4. Commercials are often in bad taste 45.5
5. Commercials claim too much for the product .. 60.1

The interrelations of these five items were:

	1	2	3	4	5
1	x	.1328	.1068	.0860	.0885
2		x	.0998	.0922	.0812
3			x	.0724	.0720
4				x	.0777
5					x

The pattern is not perfect, but there is a general tendency for Comment 1 to have higher relationships with the rest of the comments than Comment 2 has; similarly, on the average, Comment 2 is more closely related to the others than is 3, 3 than 4, and 4 than 5. This establishes that, to a considerable extent, the five comments express one basic attitude to which they are related with different degrees of closeness as shown by the order of items in the table.

The next problem is to find out, for each comment, what proportion of the people endorsing it have this general critical attitude toward commercials. Comments made more exclusively by the generally critical group may be called more severe than comments which are often agreed to by people who don't have a generally critical attitude.

The order shown by the table does not give us the order of "severity," but only the order of relationship to the general attitude. That relationship is determined by two factors —not only how few *uncritical* people agree with the particular comment, but how many of the *critical* people do agree with it. We are not now interested in the latter question, but only in the first since that is our definition of severity. A series of mathematical computations, which cannot be described here, gives us the proportion of people endorsing each comment who are generally critical of commercials:

2 Noisy .92	4 Taste .85	1 Boring .85	3 Interrupt .78	5 Claims .76

The most severe comment is that commercials are noisy since 92 per cent of those who say this are generally critical; the least severe is that they claim too much, with only 76 per cent of those who say this having a generally critical attitude.

So far we have talked only of the proportion of people having or not having a generally critical attitude. Now we must take into consideration *degrees* of this attitude. Those who agree with a given comment may have a variety of degrees of general dislike, ranging from very great dislike to no general dislike at all. We will assume that the people making a comment are distributed along a scale of general liking–disliking, in what is called a normal distribution. Each comment will have such a distribution curve, and each distribution will have an average location on the scale of liking–disliking. Now, knowing for each comment the proportion of its supporters who fall on the generally critical side of the scale, we can estimate where on the scale the average of its supporters group falls. (We do this with the help of the "table of the normal curve," which is found in any elementary statistics textbook.) This converts the *proportions* given above into *measures* of the severity of each comment. A comment which is just as likely to be answered by non-critical as by critical people is given a severity score of zero, whereas if over 97.7 per cent of a comment's supporters have the general attitude of criticism, we give it a score of 100 (in statistical terms, we give twice the standard deviation an index value of 100). It can be seen from Graph II in the text (p. 70) that each comment lies between these two limits. This specific index value is the final measure of severity.

APPENDIX F

SOME OBSERVATIONS ON
SINGING COMMERCIALS

In many ways, singing commercials have come to symbolize the controversy over radio advertising. Some consider them an improvement over the dry exposition of a radio announcer; others hold them a sign of all that is wrong with commercial radio. The controversy becomes all the more interesting when we find that listeners are fairly evenly divided in their opinion. As Table 31 indicates, the people who prefer singing commercials are almost as numerous as those who like them less well.

APPENDIX TABLE 31

"How do you feel about singing commercials? In general, do you like them better than straight commercials, or not as well?"

Better than straight commercials.................	37%
Not as well......................................	43
No difference....................................	18
Don't know......................................	2
	100%

Considering only the listeners who find some difference between jingles and straight commercials, we find that 47 per cent prefer singing commercials, whereas 53 per cent prefer the more standard type of announcement.

Such a division of opinion is always a welcome challenge in research, for it means that one can try, by further analysis, to find out what makes people hold one view rather than another. There seem to be two major factors entering into preferences for singing commercials:

Appreciation of marketing information and advice
Serious-mindedness

Singing commercials must be something of a disappointment to people who want radio advertising to tell them about the merits and qualities of different products. They are necessarily limited in their factual information; they focus on attention-getting devices; the singing voices are often indistinct. For reasons such as these, a singing commercial is not a particularly good vehicle for information. On the other hand, they are frequently more amusing than straight commercials. They often have catchy tunes, amusing sound effects, and so on. Listeners who are especially interested in entertainment, then, will probably prefer them to the standard type of commercial announcement.

It so happens that we can test this. The reader will recall that there were two positive statements about commercials among those discussed earlier that are of particular relevance here.[1] One of these said that "commercials give useful information about things you may want to buy"; the other stated that "commercials are often amusing and entertaining."[2] These two statements permit us to isolate different types of respondents. Those listeners who endorsed the first statement but disagreed with the second seem particularly interested in the information value of radio advertising; we expect, therefore, that their attitudes toward singing com-

---

[1] See Chapter IV, p. 73.

[2] It will be noted that in these two statements the respondent is asked whether he agrees that commercials *are* informative and entertaining. He is not asked specifically whether he *wants* to be informed or entertained. However, there is very probably a high correlation between the two: People who say that commercials are informative probably also want to be informed.

mercials will be especially negative. The respondents who say that commercials are entertaining but not informative will hardly be disappointed by singing commercials. We do not expect them to be so critical of jingles. These expectations are borne out by the data reported in Table 32.

APPENDIX TABLE 32

PREFERENCE FOR SINGING COMMERCIALS ACCORDING TO ENTERTAINMENT AND INFORMATION VALUE OF ADVERTISING

Radio commercials are:

Like singing commercials:	Informative, but not Entertaining	Entertaining, but not Informative	All Respondents
Better than straight	35%	46%	47%
Not as well	65	54	53
	100%	100%	100%

Attitudes toward singing commercials are influenced by a second and related factor—serious-mindedness. The demand for more educational programs, which we use here as an index of serious-mindedness, is associated with a stronger preference for the standard or straight commercial.

This same result turns up in another connection. When we examine the program types whose devotees prefer singing commercials, we find that they are programs which would be objectively classified as less serious: Hillbilly music, serials, mystery programs, quiz shows, and the like. When, on the other hand, we examine the program types whose devotees prefer standard commercial announcements, we find that they would be classified, objectively, as more serious radio fare: Classical music, forums on public issues, news programs.

The influence of serious-mindedness is reflected still

APPENDIX TABLE 33

PREFERENCE FOR SINGING COMMERCIALS
ACCORDING TO PURPOSE IN LISTENING

Like singing commercials:	Listen Mostly for Entertainment	Like Both, Now Satisfied With Programs	Want More Serious Programs
Better than straight.	51%	48%	39%
Not as well........	49	52	61
	100%	100%	100%

further in age and educational differences in attitudes toward
singing commercials. The young people and the less well
educated ones are, we know, fairly uninterested in serious

APPENDIX TABLE 34

PREFERENCE FOR SINGING COMMERCIALS
ACCORDING TO AGE AND EDUCATION*

Per cent who prefer singing commercials

	EDUCATION		
Age:	Grade School	High School	College
21–29..........	67%	58%	52%
30–49.........	58	44	34
50 and over.....	45	35	35

* Only those who express a preference for one or the other kind of commercial
are included here. Those who said they saw "no difference" between them and those
who answered "Don't know" are not considered.

matters but quite interested in entertainment. Accordingly, they more frequently prefer singing commercials.

There is one final observation on the role of radio listening in attitudes toward singing commercials. It turns out that it is only the avid fans, those who listen three hours or more on an average evening, who show any marked preference for jingles. The light and the medium listeners show very similar attitudes, and for that reason they have been grouped together in Table 35.

Why is it that fans show these preferences for singing commercials, even when they are separated into different educational groups? One might speculate that they look on singing commercials as a welcome relief from the standard commercial announcements which they hear so frequently. Because of their heavy exposure, they look for variety which is provided by the musical jingle.

One further characteristic of the heavy listeners is what might be called their greater "discrimination." As we see in Table 35, not only do they more frequently prefer singing commercials but they are also less likely to say that there is "no difference" between various types of presentation. Through their greater exposure to radio advertising, they develop very definite tastes and preferences. This, of course, is not the first time that such a relationship between experience and opinion has been found. Similar results are frequently uncovered in marketing studies: Smokers are more discriminating than nonsmokers about brands of cigarettes; women are more discriminating than men about types of cosmetics; and so on. The same relationship with regard to radio listening may be more surprising to some readers. The sophisticated minority of the radio audience, those who do most of the talking and writing about radio, are sometimes inclined to think of the radio fan as a person who lacks discrimination of any sort, even on such relatively unsophisticated questions as the distinction between singing and straight commercials.

The listeners who prefer singing commercials can thus

APPENDIX TABLE 35

PREFERENCE FOR SINGING COMMERCIALS ACCORDING TO AMOUNT OF EVENING LISTENING AND EDUCATION

	COLLEGE		HIGH SCHOOL		GRADE SCHOOL	
Like singing commercials:	Light Listeners	Heavy Listeners	Light Listeners	Heavy Listeners	Light Listeners	Heavy Listeners
Better than straight..........	31%	44%	37%	46%	37%	51%
Not as well..................	52	50	47	40	38	32
No difference................	17	6	16	14	25	17
	100%	100%	100%	100%	100%	100%

be characterized in the following way: They have a less sober outlook on life and are interested in radio primarily as a source of entertainment rather than of information. They come from social groups which produce these different interests and attitudes.

INDEX

INDEX